D0765249

56018-852 11-77 50M ① ◊ OSP

Twayne's United States Authors Series

EDITOR OF THIS VOLUME

Lewis Leary

University of North Carolina, Chapel Hill

Richard Malcolm Johnston

TUSAS 314

Richard Malcolm Johnston

RICHARD MALCOLM JOHNSTON

By BERT HITCHCOCK
Auburn University

TWAYNE PUBLISHERS
A DIVISION OF G. K. HALL & CO., BOSTON

Published in 1978 by Twayne Publishers,
A Division of G. K. Hall & Co.
All Rights Reserved

Printed on permanent/durable acid-free paper and bound
in the United States of America

First Printing

Library of Congress Cataloging in Publication Data

Hitchcock, Bert.
Richard Malcolm Johnston.

(Twayne's United States authors series ; TUSAS 314)
Bibliography: p. 153 - 59
Includes index.
1. Johnston, Richard Malcolm, 1822 - 1898. 2. Authors,
American—19th century—Biography.
PS2148.H5   813'.4   78-19049
ISBN 0-8057-7238-3

For
all the pedagogical Hitchcocks
and for
Eric,
age five,
who still prefers Joel Chandler Harris

Contents

About the Author

Bert Hitchcock is Associate Professor and Head of the Department of English at Auburn University, Auburn, Alabama. He holds a B.A. degree from Auburn, M.A. from the University of Oregon, and Ph.D. from Duke University. As a Rotary Foundation Fellow, he also attended the University of Melbourne in Australia. He serves now on the board of directors of the National Council of Teachers of English and on the executive committees of the Alabama Council of Teachers of English, Association of College English Teachers of Alabama, Alabama Council on the Teaching of Composition, Southern Humanities Conference, and Conference on College Composition and Communication. As a member of the Bibliography Committee of the Society for the Study of Southern Literature, he has contributed since 1971 to the annual "Checklist of Scholarship on Southern Literature" in the *Mississippi Quarterly*. His publications include book reviews in the *Southern Humanities Review* and "Walt Whitman: The Pedagogue as Poet" in the *Walt Whitman Review*.

Preface

At least two of the notions which visited me in the course of preparing this study have become such mental fixtures that they beg for introduction.

One has been particularly haunting. I had never "really" doubted Herman Melville's supposition that "all subjects are infinite," but I see now that I gave notional rather than real assent to that profound recognition. That many subjects were infinite I did not doubt. That Richard Malcolm Johnston was one of them, I did. I do so no longer. Loath to release so unfinished and incomplete a study, I realize now too, however, that if "it is hard to be finite upon an infinite subject," it is necessary to be so.

What has seemed the difficulty of the task has inevitably raised questions about its necessity. While I've come to view Richard Malcolm Johnston as an infinite subject, I have not changed my initial view of him as a writer of considerably less than infinite talent, and this assessment and its consequences were often in my mind. Listening to critiques and reading reviews of lengthy published treatments of minor writers, I have often been in agreement with some of the harsher opinions expressed about such efforts. I hardly need say that I have convinced myself that this concurrence always proceeded from a well-founded recognition of excessive claims and unwarranted proportions. As I come now to see the matter from the other side, however, I especially hope that I have not been deluded. I am keenly aware that the world can go on without knowing more about Richard Malcolm Johnston, but, I must say, my faith in the quality of that going on will be strengthened by an assurance that someone would like to know.

The inclusion of Johnston in the Twayne's United States Authors Series is, to me, ample testimony to this series' sincerity in seeking to promote an understanding of the American literary and cultural heritage. For if Johnston is not a major writer, as he assuredly is not, he is a writer who is important and valuable within this important and valuable framework. My hope is that this volume will be an informative introduction as well as a useful and authoritative reference work about the man and his work.

My organization of content follows directly from these aims. Using the simple and familiar if potentially misleading dichotomy of "life" and "works," I have tried to achieve a format that would facilitate the use and thus increase the true utility of the book. Chapter 1 is given over to biography. Johnston's life has not received much scholarly attention, certainly not nearly as much as is needed for a person whose life and personality, as it has been claimed, may be of more import and interest than his works. The life in this case is important also, however, for elucidating the works; for a nostalgic local colorist whose professorial prose was often denominational, biographical facts are critical in several ways and senses. Chapters 2 through 5 are devoted directly to his works. Chapter 2 considers *Dukesborough Tales*, deservedly the best-known of Johnston's productions; Chapter 3 provides a characterizing if brief look at all of the remaining tales and sketches; Chapter 4 is concerned with the novels; and Chapter 5 takes up the large quantity of nonfiction produced by this person who had a fundamental scholarly bent and a basic distrust of humorous fiction. Not simply a nod to Johnston's classical literariness, Chapter 6 is a coda, a final short assessment of the place of local color and the place of Richard Malcolm Johnston in American literary history.

As must always be the case, there are a number of individuals without whose professional or personal help this book could never have been realized. My confidence in "the community of scholarship" has been deepened immeasurably by the courteous and concerned assistance that has been given me by library after library and by one curator of manuscripts or archivist after another. To those individuals who on behalf of their institutions met my needs so willingly and so well, whether I was there in person or making exorbitant requests by mail, I am deeply grateful. To the following libraries which have given me permission to quote from unpublished manuscripts in their collections, I have a double debt of gratitude: Library of Congress; Georgia Historical Society; Columbia University; the Enoch Pratt Library, Baltimore; Duke University; the Watkinson Library, Trinity College; New York Public Library; the Lilly Library, Indiana University; and Louisiana State University.

I want also to express appreciation to Professors Arlin Turner and Louis Budd of Duke University and W. R. Patrick and Eugene Current-García of Auburn University, former mentors who have been encouraging and instrumental in this study in more ways than several. To Auburn University I have multiple indebtedness for support of my work: formally, with two research grants-in-aid and a leave of absence for research and writing, and informally, with a collection of bright, sympathetic colleagues and a departmental atmosphere congenial to scholarly pursuits. To two of my colleagues, Miller Solomon and Dennis Rygiel, who read and commented on my manuscript, I owe special thanks; had time and tact allowed, they would have made for us all a superbly readable book. And to Robin White, whose ability to reproduce readable typed copy from my script is little short of amazing, I am also grateful.

The patience of my wife has exceeded amazement. Some other compensation must be made, but for weekend and holiday worktime far in excess of what I had a right to ask, let me here record loving thanks.

BERT HITCHCOCK

Auburn University

Chronology

1822   Born March 8 at "Oak Grove," near Powelton, in Hancock County, Georgia; son of Catherine and Malcolm Johnston.

1837   Formal preparatory education completed at Powelton Academy.

1839   Entered Mercer University.

1841   Graduated from Mercer; began teaching school in Mt. Zion, Georgia.

1843   Admitted to bar after short study in Augusta; law practice begun as partner of Eli Baxter in Sparta, Georgia.

1844   Married Mary Frances Mansfield of Sparta.

1845 - 1847   Headmaster at Mt. Zion Academy.

1847 - 1849   Law practice as partner of James Thomas in Sparta.

1849 - 1851   Schoolmaster at Sparta Academy.

1852? - 1857   Law practice as partner of Linton Stephens in Sparta.

1857   Refusal of circuit judgeship and presidency of Mercer University; acceptance of professorship of belles lettres and oratory at Franklin College (The University of Georgia); "Five Chapters of a History" published in *Porter's Spirit of the Times.*

1858 - 1861   Faculty member at University of Georgia, Athens; *The English Classics*, a textbook, published (1860).

1862 - 1867   Conducted private boarding school, "Rockby," near Sparta; appointed to special wartime staff of Governor Joseph E. Brown (1862); *Georgia Sketches* published (1864).

1867   Moved with family to just outside Baltimore, Maryland; began operation of "Pen Lucy" school.

1871   *Dukesborough Tales* (Baltimore: Turnbull Brothers).

1872   [With William Hand Browne] *English Literature.*

1873   Summer trip to Europe.

1874   *Dukesborough Tales*, "Second Enlarged Edition" (Baltimore: Turnbull Brothers). Summer trip to Europe.

1875   Conversion to Roman Catholicism.

1878   [With William Hand Browne] *Life of Alexander H. Stephens.*

1879   First paid story, "Mr. Neelus Peeler's Conditions," published in *Scribner's Monthly Magazine.*

1883   Pen Lucy school closed; moved family into Baltimore and began attempt to become a professional man of letters. *Dukesborough Tales* (New York: Harper & Brothers).

1884   *Old Mark Langston.*

1885   *Two Gray Tourists.*

1888   *Mr. Absalom Billingslea and Other Georgia Folk.*

1889   *Ogeechee Cross-Firings.*

1890   *Widow Guthrie.*

1891   *The Primes and Their Neighbors. Studies, Literary and Social,* First Series.

1892   *Mr. Billy Downs and His Likes. Mr. Fortner's Marital Claims and Other Stories. Studies, Literary and Social,* Second Series. *Dukesborough Tales: The Chronicles of Mr. Bill Williams* (New York: D. Appleton).

1894   *Little Ike Templin and Other Stories.*

1895   Appointed to position in United States Department of Labor; received Doctor of Laws degrees from St. Mary's Seminary (Baltimore) and the University of Notre Dame (Indiana).

1896   Began work in United States Bureau of Education.

1897   Death of Mary Frances Mansfield Johnston. *Old Times in Middle Georgia. Lectures on Literature: English, French and Spanish.* Received honorary doctorate from the University of Georgia.

1898   *Pearce Amerson's Will.* Died September 23 in Baltimore.

1900   *Autobiography of Colonel Richard Malcolm Johnston,* posthumously published.

CHAPTER 1

The Gentlemanly and Uncertain Worlds of Law, Learning, and Literature

I F, as one of his daughters remarked, Richard Malcolm Johnston's personality was greater than his writings, a knowledge of his life may be more important than a knowledge of his works. Of course, lives and personalities and literary works are not neatly separable, and to suggest such a segregation in the case of a nostalgic local colorist signals, to use a phrase of Johnston's, the "dereliction of understanding."

Whatever the line of justification, there is, however, special need for delineation of the facts of this man's life. Partly because he was so late coming into public view and partly because he displayed then such a pleasing personality, the facts have not been ferreted out. The full, objective biography both urged and prevented by Johnston's impressive personal presence has yet to be written.[1]

I Middle Georgia Seedtime (1822 - 1858)

Richard Malcolm Johnston, the next to youngest of the six children of Catherine and Malcolm Johnston, was born March 8, 1822, at "Oak Grove," the Johnston family homeplace four miles west of the village of Powelton in Hancock County, Georgia. Malcolm Johnston, fond of talking to his children about their forebears, could go as far back as his grandfather, the Anglican clergyman Thomas Johnston, who had emigrated from Scotland to Pennsylvania. Moving southward, the Reverend Mr. Johnston lived first in Maryland and then in Charlotte County, Virginia. His oldest child, William, continued the southern movement, settling what was to become "Oak Grove" in 1799. Malcolm, who was William's youngest son, was born in Virginia, but he put deep roots into the

15

Georgia soil. And Malcolm's youngest son, Richard Malcolm, although he was to reverse the family movement and return to Maryland, had even deeper roots in Middle Georgia, roots that would support a remarkable literary flowering in his old age.

Malcolm Johnston, who was born in 1788, loomed large in several respects. He was a big man physically, standing six feet tall and weighing well over two hundred pounds. And, although the Johnstons were not the aristocratic plantation family of Old South myth, Malcolm Johnston's holdings and influence gave him rather high position in the democratic society of Middle Georgia. From sixteen slaves and three hundred acres of land ten years before Richard was born, he came finally to own around sixty slaves and a plantation of 2,500 acres. For some years before and for several after 1822, Malcolm Johnston was, as his son said in his autobiography, "an active, ardent, rather gay man" who was fond of poker and dancing parties, of fox-hunting and morning toddies. Then came a revolutionary religious conversion, which was formalized by membership in the Baptist Church. Later, Baptist leader Jesse Mercer, in keeping with his inspired practice of making preachers of prominent Georgia planters, persuaded Malcolm Johnston to become a Baptist clergyman. Mr. Johnston's Masonic activity and leadership were readily transformed into church activity and leadership. Serving on the Executive Committee of the Georgia Baptist Convention, he was especially active in support of and solicitation for the institution that was to become Mercer University, and he was in the very first group of trustees elected for that school in 1838. Not surprising for a man who was paid less than twenty-five dollars in cash for twenty years of preaching is what is reported to have been a pet remark of. Malcolm Johnston's: "the best, safest bank in the world is a clay-bank, and the best share in it is a plough-share."[2]

Although his planter father would clearly appear in some of his son's local-color sketches, it was probably his mother who was the strongest influence on Richard Malcolm, both as a boy and as a man. Catherine Smith Davenport Johnston, eight years the senior of Malcolm, married him after the death of her first husband, Henry Byrom, whose land adjoined that of Mr. Johnston. Her memorable blue eyes Richard Malcolm inherited, but probably the twinkle in them was more a paternal legacy. Mrs. Catherine Johnston, quiet and rather melancholy, provided a contrast to her more cheerful and outgoing husband. The sensitive Richard and his mother were extremely close, practicing until her death in September of 1842 the expressive ritual of his laying his head in her lap and having his hair tenderly fondled.

The home life presided over by these parents was a combination of strictest discipline and tenderest affection, of somber, meditative Sundays and cheerful, busy weekdays. Richard Malcolm was, by his own account, a frail and sickly child for whom reading was an early acquisition and books an early love. His formal education, and the long line of schoolmasters he would remember both as a writer and as an educator, began when he was five years old. Going with his brother Mark to a rural "old-field" school, he was rudely brought to the feast of learning—or, more aptly, the scraps—by a man named Hogg. Josiah Yellowby, wife-dominated and on one occasion student-dominated, succeeded Hogg in the pedagogical chair, and Yellowby was in turn succeeded by James Hilsman, who delighted in corporal punishment.

In 1831 Malcolm Johnston, evidently aware of what his children were getting and not getting in school, left his overseer in charge of his plantation and moved his family ten miles to Crawfordville. Here, in a school kept by a well-educated South Carolinean, Richard Malcolm was introduced to Latin, but he made little progress in that study until the family moved to Powelton in 1834 and he was enrolled in the academy there. Under Lucian Whittle, a native of Vermont, young Richard learned Latin and Greek and was, by the end of 1837, prepared to enter the last half of second-year university studies. Returning with his family to "Oak Grove," he entered into something quite different, however.

Relating in his autobiography his everpresent fear of punishment and his great anxiety over school lessons, Johnston attributed his slow physical growth and his continuing frail heath at this time to his uninterrupted ten years of school attendance. This idea was probably first his father's, who took remedial action, then extremely irksome but later much appreciated by his son. This action—"this discipline," as Richard Malcolm called it—consisted of a weekly dose of four days of hard field labor with the slaves; two days, Friday and Saturday, were free for hunting or other activities. As a result, although still sensitive and unsure of himself and still very credulous and naive, a robust and healthy Richard set off in February, 1839, for Mercer University, located then at Penfield, Georgia, about twenty miles away.

Set up on a Swiss model, Mercer was at this time a manual-labor school, requiring in addition to attendance upon its academic program two hours a day of physical labor. Although Mercer Institute had been in operation since 1833, Mercer University and Richard Malcolm Johnston were both making a new start with the school year of 1839. In this year, there were eighty-one academy students and, for the first time, fourteen college matriculants; the next year, 1840, saw 132 students in the academic and collegiate departments and a professorial faculty of six.[3] The junior and senior year courses of study, through which Johnston passed with ease, were advertised as including Natural Philosophy, Engineering, Conic Sections, Spherical Geometry and Trigonometry, Natural History, Logic, Criticism, Rhetoric, Evidences of Christianity, Natural Theology, Astronomy, Chemistry, Moral Philosophy, Mental Philosophy, Practical Economy, American Constitution, and the Classics—also "Frequent Exercise in Composition and Declamation."[4] Johnston joined the Phi Delta Society at Mercer and was soon recognized as a leading debater at its Saturday morning sessions. He also sang in the school choir. By July of 1841, the new university was ready to award its first baccalaureate degrees, and by virtue of alphabetization, its very first went to Richard Malcolm Johnston—Benjamin F. Tharpe and Abner R. Wellborn constituting the remainder of the class.[5]

Johnston, who would later serve on Mercer University's board of trustees, but who turned down two other offers which would have brought him back to Mercer, was grateful for the increased self-confidence that his college years had given him. Fifty years later, though unsure of how much he had truly "ripened," he remembered clearly the day when as a "green" youth, dressed in buff trousers and vest, and a blue half dress coat with large buttons, he spoke a sad valedictory at Mercer's first graduation.[6]

Poverty is the mother of wind-selling lawyers, "the Necessity which knows no Law, yet teaches so much of it," wrote Joseph G. Baldwin in *The Flush Times of Alabama and Mississippi* (1853). Many an ambitious son of many a middleclass Southern planter chose to pursue the law for more positive reasons, however, and if, in fact, necessity procured for any one occupation more than for another in nineteenth-century America, this vocation was schoolteaching. Necessity first made Richard Malcolm Johnston a schoolmaster, political ambition probably then making him seek admission to the bar. For over ten years, though, he was to vacillate between the two professions, sometimes practicing them concurrently but most often switching back and forth between the two. Finally the decision was made for teaching. During all of his uncertainty about vocation, however, Johnston was to be abidingly constant to two commitments: to his wife, "Fanny," whom he married in 1844, and to another object of deep love, literature.

To the vocation in which he was first to achieve widespread reputation Johnston had first "almost to be driven by my father and urged by other friends." Because Malcolm Johnston had had to contribute to the support of the families of his two eldest, married daughters, Richard Malcolm Johnston had to put his college education to initial use in schoolkeeping, as it then was called. Immediately after his graduation from Mercer, he took over a school at Mt. Zion, a little village in Hancock County, where after a rather traumatic but maturing beginning, he was master for about a year and a half. At Mt. Zion he also did a little private tutoring. Having read Sir William Blackstone's *Commentaries* during the last year of this tenure, Johnston set off for Augusta at the end of 1842 to study law. Here he worked in the law office of Henry Cumming, attended the lectures of William Tracy Gould, and within two months was admitted to the bar. He returned to Hancock County, to the county seat of Sparta, and was taken into partnership by Eli Baxter. For the next two years, however, his legal activities were mostly of a clerical nature. Almost all of his leisure time, he later said, was spent reading English and Latin literature.

In 1844 Johnston received his Master's degree from Mercer and decided to go back again to schoolteaching. Most important, however, on November 26 he married Mary Frances ("Fanny") Mansfield, the bright, attractive fifteen-year-old daughter of Eli Mansfield, a Connecticut native who had become a resident of Sparta. Letters from Eli Mansfield's niece, Mary Ann Mansfield, to her family back in Connecticut are full of praise both for her cousin "Fanny" and for Fanny's intended, "Dick" Johnston.[7] Mary Mansfield, who had arrived in Sparta in September, 1838, hoping for a teaching position, wrote to her father on October 22 about nine-year-old Fanny's new violin, only one of four instruments that she played. She "is a very good scholar in her English studies and a superior one in her music," reported the older cousin. Writing to her sister on August 13 of the following year, Mary Ann Mansfield confirmed her now firm opinion of Fanny, who, she wrote, "is an uncommon smart child, as is acknowledged by every one acquainted with her." Obviously, Johnston was sufficiently acquainted and uncommonly impressed. "The talk is," Mary Ann Mansfield could communicate to New Haven five years later, on November 20, 1844, "Fanny is to be married the 26th of this month to a young lawyer in Hancock. I am but slighty acquainted with this gentleman, Mr. Johnson [*sic*] except by reputation. He is talented, correct in his morals, energetic and industrious." "So far as I am able to judge," she reported from the Mansfield family perspective, "he is worthy of her in every respect." The only possible objection to the "alliance" that Mary Ann Mansfield could think of was Fanny's "extreme youth," but, as Johnston himself later took pains to point out, fifteen was not an unusual age for a Georgia girl to be married.

In letters to friends twenty-five and then fifty years later, Johnston (who signed himself "Richard" in the letters he wrote his young wife) lovingly recounted the events of that crisp, sunshiny November day in 1844 when he and Fanny were married.[8] Particularly did he recall the large wedding party at his father's house, which celebrated with much music and merriment the marriage that had earlier been solemnized in Sparta, fifteen miles distant. The union was to endure for more than fifty-two years. Not free of some strains and strife, of some crispness along with the sunshine, it was remarkably durable, probably more because of Johnston's nature than anything else. Johnston allowed his spouse to exercise a great deal of influence over him. Possibly it was the dictate of wisdom, for Fanny Johnston, it was said, showed her New England ancestry in her temper as well as in her strong-willed independence and self-reliance, her intellectual curiosity and sharpness, and her passionate religious devoutness. Quieter and more pensive than her husband, she relished privacy as much as he did society. Perhaps more esthetically sensitive, she was definitely a more efficient manager and shrewder judge of business than he. She fussed at him about his drinking, his disheveled appearance, his credulity, and his absentmindedness, but she bore Richard Malcolm twelve children, nine of whom lived into maturity. Though she clearly felt herself a martyr to marriage at times, she must also have felt the love that made her grieving husband inscribe a book four months after her death, "To Frances Mansfield Johnston, Who being dead yet lives."[9]

By early in 1845, Dick Johnston had returned to schoolkeeping and to Mt. Zion, having accepted the headship of the academy there. Boarding at Mr. Neal's with his young wife, who was teaching music, he had forty to fifty pupils in his school and, according to Mary Ann Mansfield, appeared "very well satisfied with himself and every one around him."[10] He was still also practicing a little law at this time, perhaps meeting earlier commitments, and was already referred to as "Colonel" Johnston. In keeping with a common practice of the time and locale, the title was probably given him by friends and colleagues soon after he came to the bar.

Johnston continued at Mt. Zion for two years, and although the academic prospects there were good, in December, 1846, he and Fanny moved the six miles back to Sparta, where he again began to practice law and entered a new partnership, this time with James Thomas. He resolved to study the law industriously this time, and read and took notes "constantly" for three years; but while his learning was admired by his colleagues, his inability to function before juries was the envy of no one. This "infirmity" increased to the point of his suffering intense anxiety before the beginning of court sessions, and taking advantage of Mr. Thomas's retirement in 1849, he took once more to schoolkeeping, this time at the academy in Sparta. This period of teaching lasted only two years, for when his lawyer friend Linton Stephens married James Thomas's widowed daughter and moved to Sparta, Johnston "came back," as he says, to the practice of law. He was to be back, this time, for six years.

Johnston's formal association with the younger half-brother of Alexander H. Stephens lasted from probably early 1852 until the end of 1857. Begun on a basis of respect and admiration, it became much more than a law partnership, though that arrangement, too, was a satisfactory one. Between the two young men, Johnston the elder by a year, developed a rare enriching sympathy and strong mutual attachment. Linton Stephens, said Johnston, became "unspeakably dear" to him in the twenty years of their intimate "never-interrupted" friendship, broken only by Stephens's death in 1872.[11] It was the first and perhaps the profoundest of the significant friendships that Johnston seemed especially equipped to engender and experience.[12] Although Mrs. Stephens died in 1857, the 1850s were busy and in general good and happy years for the two young lawyers and their families. Each man during this time passed thirty years of age, and each was beginning to achieve some reputation in the wider world. Already commissioned with his gratuitous colonelcy, Johnston began now to see the premature whitening of his hair; thus two "trademarks" of his later Southern gentleman image seem early to have been established. But more important foundations were also being laid during this period.

Richard Malcolm Johnston of the firm of Stephens and Johnston was engaged in literary, political, and educational as well as legal activities. The professional agreement he had with Linton Stephens permitted a naturally complementary division of the practice. Johnston, who liked the scholarly, research aspects of preparing a case, did not like speaking publicly before a court, which was, however, what his partner did like. "Linton and I suit one another well I think," said Johnston in a May 14, 1856, letter to Alexander Stephens; "at least he suits me exactly, as he is always ready to do that portion of our duties which is the most irksome to me."[13] His law practice was what supported Johnston's family, but the law circuit in general and his arrangement and association with Stephens in particular supported another pursuit, the creation of literature.

In the same May, 1856, letter to Stephens, Johnston had specified why he was so pleased with his present situation. "My tastes and habits," he wrote, "have always been more for a literary than a professional career." Released from the most distasteful (to him) requirements of his profession, he could now find "some time for the cultivation of letters, which the circumstances of my life heretofore have not encouraged; and I am anxious to do something in the line of life for which I have always felt myself the best fitted." And, he added in a revealing and what would become an ironic afterthought, "Not that I hope that with the very best advantage & encouragement, I could achieve any considerable reputation, but that my own being would be advanced the best by such a pursuit." He had already at this time, as a matter of fact, begun the pursuit. He used his acquaintance with some of the literati of Augusta to correspond with *the* literary man of Charleston, William Gilmore Simms. From Sparta he wrote on December 5, 1855, to inquire if it would be possible to become a contributor to Simms's *Southern Quarterly Review*, explaining that he was "anxious to devote a part of my time to the cultivation of letters."[14] This hopeful inquiry concerned an article on religious and political history, but articles were not all the scholarly lawyer was writing in his "leisure from professional duties." This article ultimately appeared in *DeBow's Review* in 1857, but that same year the more widely circulated *Porter's Spirit of the Times* published a Johnston "essay" of quite another kind, a delightful and humorous local-color sketch entitled "Five Chapters of a History."

This was the tale that would eventually be called "The Goosepond School," and its participation in the literary tradition of Old Southwestern humor was as plain as the connection between this humor and the old law circuits of the region. In Middle Georgia, according to Joel Chandler Harris, "character and individuality ran riot, appearing in such strange and attractive shapes as to puzzle and bewilder even those who were familiar with the queer manifestations."[15] No one was more familiar, no one more delightedly puzzled and bewildered, no one more willing to try to articulate all of these manifestations than the lawyers who rode the court circuits. In the various crowded little taverns of courthouse towns at court time, as one of them recalled, "assembled at night the rollicking boys of the Georgia Bar, who here indulged, without restraint, the convivialities for which they were so celebrated. Humor and wit, in anecdotes and repartee, beguiled the hours; and the few old taverns time has spared, could they speak, might narrate more good things their walls have heard, than have ever found record in the *Noctes Ambrosianae* of the wits of Scrogie."[16] These excellent raconteurs of the bar knew the people intimately, said Johnston, and, as he too recollected, they would at the periodic reunions of the brotherhood spend hour upon nocturnal hour "in story-tellings about their neighbors, friends, one another, and even themselves, to be followed by shouts [of laughter] that . . . would be heard throughout the village. . . ."[17] The general predilection and collective pastime were evidenced more specifically when only Johnston and Stephens were together. "I never expect to enjoy again such raciness of talk as we used to have in that library when we would all get warmed in contact," said Johnston in recalling visits to his partner's home. "There was many a character, both in Hancock, and the adjoining counties, whose oddities he and I well knew, and the rehearsal of their doings and sayings would be followed by shouts of laughter that it would be glorious to hear and to utter."[18] Given this environment, such an eminent and successful lawyer-teacher-writer predecessor as A. B. Longstreet, and Johnston's own attraction to the cultivation of letters, it is not surprising that he might want to rehearse, to utter, on a larger stage.

The practice of law had, of course, long been considered a stage for politics, a rehearsal for the achievement and performances of public office. Johnston reports in his autobiography the active political as well as religious partisanship of his father, and the son, who was to follow suit on both counts, followed the political lead first. He reports of himself that "during the first four or five years after coming to the bar I took active interest in politics, not infrequently taking the stump." Becoming embroiled in disputes threatening serious consequences and once only narrowly escaping a duel, Johnston finally forswore such active partisan political participation. "In time," as he puts it in the autobiography, "I discovered that I was of too ardent a temper for a politician."

Although this "time" for discovery may have been the four or five years that Johnston seems to claim, his "active interest in politics" in Georgia extended to more nearly fourteen or fifteen years. His close association with Linton Stephens may have rekindled some interest after a period of uncertainty, but Johnston's later statement in his autobiography that he had "never been active in politics" is misleading if not false. Young Colonel Johnston was known to Mary Ann Mansfield in 1844 as an ardent Democrat who spoke handsomely in public on that party's behalf, and he himself reports his attendance at a Democratic mass meeting in Macon in August, 1844. He was active enough in the campaign of 1855 to react strongly and directly to the new anti-foreigner, anti-Catholic Know-Nothing Party (three related articles he wrote for the *Constitutionalist*, a Democratic party organ, were reworked into an 1857 *DeBow's Review* piece), and he himself ran for a circuit judgeship in 1857.

This one foray into political candidacy saw him defeated by Garnett Andrews, the Know-Nothing gubernatorial candidate of 1855. Certain it is that Johnston was known personally by many of the state's leading politicians during these years, years of intense party conflict with consideration of momentous national issues, years that comprise "a sort of golden age" in Georgia's political history.[19] Conclaves and conventions of the various Georgia parties seem to have occurred incessantly, especially in the 1850s, and Richard Malcolm Johnston, with the Stephens brothers when they became Democrats, probably attended a number of appropriate ones. Johnston appears to have been a member of the committee appointed by the State Democratic Convention in 1857 to inform Joseph E. Brown that he had received the party's nomination for governor.[20] Brown, who was elected and thrice reelected, became Georgia's famous Civil War governor, an incumbency that would prove fortunate for the former news-bearing committeeman.

The clientele of his private schools in the 1860s and 1870s testify to Johnston's wide acquaintance with Georgia's influential legal and political figures in the '40s and '50s. Both the clientele and the very existence of the schools are evidence of his having also made a name for himself in the field of education. The young lawyer-schoolmaster seems to have gained at an early stage of his career a reputation as a man of culture and an effective public speaker. Evidently, Johnston was as confidently superb in delivering a prepared oration as he was miserably inept in arguing extemporaneously before judges and juries. He was invited, for example, to give Fourth of July speeches in Mt. Zion and Sparta in the 1840s, and to citizens of the latter he delivered a long public eulogy on General Zachary Taylor in 1848. In 1848 or 1849 he accepted an invitation to speak to his fellow Masons in Washington, Georgia. More and more, however, requests for Johnstonian oratory came from educational institutions and groups, and they began to come from farther and farther away.

Mercer University, especially, remembered her first graduate well and favorably. At the 1846 commencement Johnston spoke before the Phi Delta Society at Penfield, and about ten years later he addressed Mercer alumni meeting in Penfield. He was at the time of this latter appearance a member of the board of trustees of the institution, having been appointed in 1855. Also in 1855 he had been tendered but had refused the Chair of Ancient Languages at his alma mater. Probably, too, it was the Baptist-Mercer connection that secured Johnston the invitation to be commencement orator at the Georgia Female College in Madison in 1850, where he appeared on the program with William T. Brantly, Professor of Belles Lettres at Franklin College, the early name of the University of Georgia.

A reputation of sorts established, Johnston came to important personal and professional crossroads in 1857. Three prestigious positions were offered to him almost simultaneously, and his choice was the least publicly prestigious but clearly the most personally congenial of them. First, shortly after his defeat by Garnett Andrews, he was offered executive appointment to the unexpired term of Judge Eli Baxter (Johnston's former law partner). Since only six months of this tenure remained, he refused, but the election of judges having become the responsibility of the state legislature, Democrat Johnston's name was to be placed before the 1858 Democratic legislature for certain approval for the succeeding term. The second offer was that of the presidency of Mercer University, extended, rather embarrassingly for Johnston, by the board of trustees of which he was a member. The third offer, resulting from the election held by the board of trustees of the University of Georgia on August 5, was to succeed William T. Brantly in the professorship of belles lettres and oratory at that institution.

After some hesitation—several weeks' reflection, according to Johnston—he accepted the professorship. In historical perspective, the refusal of the judgeship is not surprising. It meant, as Johnston notes in his autobiography, his retirement "for good and all from a profession for which, in some of its most important and trying functions, I felt myself to be not sufficiently qualified." His reasons for not accepting the Mercer presidency are perhaps less predictable, but, if the autobiography is trustworthy, they are important presages of events in Athens and especially in Baltimore. Turning down the offer two hours after it was tendered, Johnston later explained that he did not like "the course of college discipline then obtaining everywhere." "I knew," he says, "that I could never practice over youth an espionage from which my feelings revolted." More important, however, was that Mercer "was a denominational institution with a department of theology attached." His "chief reason for declining," said Johnston, "was that, although I was a member of the Baptist Church, my trust in some of its principles had dwindled, although I had never contemplated withdrawal from it altogether. . . . I had not taken part in any of the public exercises of the congregation, and it would have much embarrassed me to lead the morning and evening prayers in the chapel."

The parting from Linton Stephens was very sad to him, but Colonel Dick Johnston was, for a while at least, to be Professor Johnston. He would later return to Hancock County for a few years, but the people and the life he had so loved there, if they had not in truth disappeared in the 1840s, would be gone forever with the tumult of the Civil War.

II   A Born Teacher Twice Removed (1858 - 1867)

A local newspaper announcing Richard M. Johnston's acceptance of the faculty position at the University of Georgia expressed the belief that a particularly fine and mutually advantageous bargain had been struck. Colonel Johnston, it stated, was the very man for the job; the professorship suited well "his literary taste and elegant scholarship," and he would prove to be, it was predicted, a most valuable acquisition for the institution at Athens.[21] While Athens historian A. L. Hull recognized that Johnston was "a student by taste," Hull's full picture of the young professor put the emphasis on his personality rather than on his scholarship. And this, according to later literary historian Edd Winfield Parks,[22] was the proper placement of emphasis. However, in 1857—as for several years before and for many thereafter—this distinction was not one which occurred to his contemporaries. If Dick Johnston had a pleasing personality, it was partly because he was impressive as a man of culture, a man of "literary taste and elegant scholarship." Although the exact description was not to come until later, he must have seemed in 1857 the type of man whom Thomas Carlyle would have called "a heaven-born teacher."[23]

Some indication of the statewide reputation that Johnston enjoyed is provided by what appears to be his first formal connection with the University of Georgia: even before assuming the professorship, he had been elected to the Demosthenian Literary Society in February, 1856. In accepting this honorary membership, Johnston joined such men of letters as Hugh Swinton Legaré, George Tucker, J. J. Hooper, William Gilmore Simms, and William Cullen Bryant. His association with the university would change, but it would endure for his lifetime. Elected a trustee a year and a half after he had resigned from the faculty, he returned to Athens to be invested with an honorary doctorate in 1897, forty years almost to the month after he had been chosen a professor.

Johnston arrived for his first term on the faculty of the university after a wet and muddy trip from Hancock County, and in the midst of a scarlet fever scare, in January, 1858. He remained four academic years—until late fall, 1861. The chair he held, with an annual salary of around $2,000, was at first officially that of Belles Lettres, Evidences of Christianity, and History. Reflecting changes dictated by Johnston's interests, he was later listed as Professor of Belles Lettres, English Literature, and History. He also taught Rhetoric and Oratory, and mentions in several letters to Alexander Stephens the demanding tasks of correcting compositions and hearing speeches. Then as now there were university committees, and Johnston did his duty in this regard, his most important committee work dealing with a reorganization of the university calendar into two terms rather than three. The college academic year ran from January through late October, although Commencement was always held in August.

Johnston's biographers have usually had three main observations to make about his professorial years. The first, based upon Johnston's emphasis in his autobiography and elsewhere, is that he had serious disagreement with and finally significantly deviated from "the course of college discipline" in force at that time. Failing

to acquaint himself very well about his duties before arriving in
Athens, he took immediate issue with professional "patrol work,"
the requirement that, within his assigned jurisdiction or "range,"
each professor was to visit each student's room each day. This sur-
veillance, and indeed the whole prevailing attitude of college discipline which made the student-teacher relationship so distrustful
and antagonistic, Johnston objected to on the grounds of the code of
gentlemanly conduct. The purpose of such rules as daily trips to student rooms, he said, was for the sake of good order, and good order
he believed would best be maintained by his absence, not by his
snooping and inconvenient presence. Before long, then, he suspended the making of these rounds, letting students know "that I did so
because I did not believe that they would take advantage of the
trust which I thus showed in their sense of propriety in response to
fair treatment. Such behavior on my part, recognizing their respect
for the amenities due and common among gentlemen everywhere,
made my life and that of my family free from molestation of any
sort."[24] Once also, according to his own testimony, he astounded
both colleagues and students by apologizing publicly to a student
whom, he felt upon reflection, he had reprimanded unjustly. Quite
concerned about student morals, Johnston believed in discipline,
but he argued for and exerted discipline under a system in which, as
he believed essential, a teacher could have some meaningful and
positive personal influence. He seems to have striven conscientious-
ly for good relationships with his students, and he did so at least in
part from some larger educational principles and from a clear, firm
idea of what a university should be.

Liberal if not revolutionary, then, in his views on this aspect of
college life, Professor Johnston was also a curriculum innovator.
Under him, as he wrote to Alexander Stephens and as the catalog of
the university verifies, English literature and English literary history
were offered for the first time at Georgia. And these subjects were
not being offered at many colleges around the country at that time.
Because he could find no suitable textbook, Johnston wrote his own,
*The English Classics: A Historical Sketch of the Literature of
England From the Earliest Times to the Accession of King George
III*, which was published by Lippincott of Philadelphia in 1860.
This book—his first—was not, however, as has been claimed, the
first American textbook on the subject, nor was Johnston, as has
been intimated, the first to offer such college courses. Still, because
"before 1860 English studies in most colleges consisted of rhetoric
and oratory, and nothing more,"[25] Johnston can legitimately be

regarded as in the vanguard of the movement. Certainly, Lippincott wasted no time in accepting his original manuscript, and a revised and enlarged edition, done in collaboration with William Hand Browne, appeared with a new publisher in 1872 and was reissued several times afterward.

The third common observation about the Athens years, one which more concerns Johnston's relations with colleagues and peers than with students, emerges from his autobiographical remembrance of great personal happiness during this period. In calling the time "almost unmixedly contented," Johnston told the truth but not the whole truth. He was very much pleased with the cordiality and hospitality of Athens, with the high state of society and culture that existed there. In the entertaining in the homes, he and Mrs. Johnston, well-liked and both accomplished musicians, were often called upon to perform. But at the college itself all was not so well.

The five years preceding the outbreak of the Civil War were "stormy and devastating ones" for the University of Georgia.[26] It had come, in fact, to its own civil war a little earlier than the nation. Friction between Alonzo Church, the conservative New Englander who had been president since 1829, and many of the professors who arrived in Athens in the 1840s and early '50s reached a climax in 1856 when the trustees called for a total mass resignation. Dr. Church and three professors were reelected, but Johnston quickly perceived after his arrival in 1858 a "continued hostility" and a continuing lack of public support for the institution. Dr. Church announced his intention to resign after the next academic year, and a rather radical reorganization proposal and some attempted reforms in admission and class honors procedures added to the turmoil of 1859. The next year—without a president—was even worse in the opinion of Professor Johnston, who felt that his own earnest efforts were unrecognized and unappreciated and that the university in general was rapidly disintegrating. "Do I look like one who is in the right place?" he queried Alexander Stephens on February 9, 1860. "Can I stay here honorably?" Having thought about resigning the year before, he did submit a resignation in May, 1860, to be effective at the end of the school year, but he agreed to delay a final decision until that time. In the meantime, A. A. Lipscomb was elected chancellor, and Lipscomb, partly by promising him an introduction to Harpers Publishers but also impressing him on less selfish grounds, induced Johnston to remain. The next year, 1861, was to be his last in Athens, however.

Johnston gave several explanations of his decision to leave the

university. In his autobiography he stressed his stand against secession, a minority and unpopular stand in Athens. And, he noted,
with the outbreak of war the university's enrollment began drop-
ping drastically. In addition, in letters to the Stephenses he pointed
specifically to his growing family and gave the inadequacy of his
professorial salary as the reason for resigning. All of these facts were
factors in his decision, but the main reason, as Alexander Stephens
and Johnston both recognized, was simply that Athens was not, had
never been, and could not be "home" for Johnston.

The four years he had spent in Athens, Johnston said toward the
end of the period, was about what he had anticipated when he
accepted the professorship. While he had not liked the internal
politics and some of the duties at the university, he had very much
liked the outlet and opportunity for his literary pursuits which he
found there. Inspired and animated by the publication of his "Five
Chapters of a History" in *Spirit of the Times*, and by its reprinting
in various newspapers around the state, Johnston spent some time
during the first two years writing and rewriting stories; later, as his
series of newspaper articles on the establishment of a university and
his *English Classics* predict and illustrate, he seems to have been
more occupied with professional matters. He also wrote for publication some short biographical sketches of Linton and Alexander H.
Stephens which, since he was scrupulous about the facts, demanded
special research.

What potentially productive spare time he may have had,
however, was severely cut into by his numerous trips away from
Athens, most often to Hancock County. Since he made these
journeys at court term to court towns, Johnston was obviously still
involved in a number of law cases, and he was also still involved in
farming. His plantation, "Kildee," near Sparta he had left in the
care of a foreman, who sent the anxious Johnston frequent and
regular reports. And to "Kildee" at each annual long vacation of the
university went the whole Johnston entourage—father, mother,
children, and domestic servants. Although he had made good
friends in Athens, they could not, Johnston believed, replace those
in his dear native Hancock, and he wrote hungrily, even desperately, for news from Sparta whenever he had, for what he considered
an inordinate time, not been able to go there for a visit. Ironically, it
was, he would say, for the sake of his family that he left Hancock
County for good in 1867, but he was going back there in 1861
because only there could his children get the *"home feelings"* he

considered "necessary in order to make [them] good men and women."[27] However, he wrote Linton Stephens, he hadn't really stopped to consider how much he had been prompted by a sense of duty to his family and how much he had been moved by "the pure longing for my native home." "I only know," he said, "that it is very sweet to think that I shall return there soon."[28]

Because he needed the money but also because he believed it was mankind's duty to labor and his specific duty to teach, since he did some good thereby, Johnston decided to open a select boarding school for boys on his Hancock plantation.[29] It was a scheme he had thought of and set afoot when resignation from the professorship was much on his mind in 1860. Erecting special buildings and calling the place "Rockby," Johnston opened his school in January, 1862, with a class of twenty boys, ages twelve to sixteen. The number exceeded not his expectations but his desire, for he had planned in terms of ten or twelve and then fifteen or sixteen pupils. Enrollment would rise as high as fifty in the five-and-a-half-year history of Rockby, and many more students than this wanted to attend.

The idea of a private school had come to Johnston from his knowledge of the well-known Beman's Academy in Mt. Zion where he had done service in the 1840s, but his own school differed significantly from this or any other such institution. Taking advantage, he said, of what he had learned as a student and a teacher, Johnston put into effect an educational and disciplinary system that, founded on his code of the gentleman, was a most humane and liberal one for its time. Declaring that he was no detective and would tolerate no espionage, Johnston placed the responsibility for their conduct directly upon the boys, stating in his advertisement for Rockby that "no pupil would be allowed to remain in the school, whose veracity should be found unworthy of confidence." His broad program of education, based on his conviction of the importance of the personal influence of a sympathetic and interested teacher and of the concomitant importance of cultivating "home feelings," Johnston expressed in a prospectus letter to Herschel V. Johnson in 1860. His plan, he said, was to take a relatively small number of boys, "to board and educate them, to take them in my house, place them upon the same footing with my children, to superintend their reading, to endeavor to form their tastes, and besides teaching them text books to give them some instruction in the elements of music. I shall teach classical and mathematical studies mostly, not intending to give much attention to the sciences, believing that they can be taught successfully only in the University."[30]

The success of Rockby is confirmed by the fine reputation that the school acquired and by the personal testimonies that Rockby pupils volunteered years later. The boys, who were allowed to take full advantage of the rural setting, not only hunted and less purposefully roamed the fields and forests of the plantation, but they often studied out-of-doors, going into the schoolroom only when it was time for their particular recitation.

The school and residence buildings were set in a beautifully landscaped enclosure planned and presided over by Mrs. Johnston, who, though as talented in gardening as she was in music, had in this case the help of P. J. Berckmans, a horticulturist of wide and justified reputation. Close to the house were hedges, rare shrubs, and all varieties of flowers, and on the outskirts were orchards of peaches, pears, and apples, and a small vineyard.

Johnston allowed his charges to play cards in public, had many special musical entertainments, and even permitted dances occasionally on Friday nights. His pupils, too, were always invited to sit in on the after-dinner conversations when the Colonel's well-known political friends came to call. The boys did indeed feel part of a large, affectionate family, and strong cords of friendship were tied among group members. Johnston spent much more than he had planned in setting up Rockby, but the rather high tuitions of around $300 to $500 allowed him some profit. With Rockby he succeeded also in his desire to keep a school in which there was "no humbug"; certainly his students seemed to profit far beyond their ability upon graduation to enter a university with junior standing.

The Rockby period was a busy one for Johnston, but with an assistant or two to help him with instruction and slaves to help with other work, he found time again for the production and publication of imaginative literature. He may have finished much of the writing before he left Athens, but in January and then March, 1863, "Five Chapters of a History: A Georgia Court, Forty Years Ago" and "The Last Day of Mr. Williamson Slippey, Salt Merchant" appeared in *Southern Field and Fireside*, one of the best antebellum periodicals in Georgia. The first story, which would finally be called "Judge Mike's Court," was soon issued in a separate novellette series by the same publisher, Stockton and Company of Augusta. More satisfying, no doubt, was the book called

Georgia Sketches which Stockton published in 1864. Issued pseudonymously, it was Johnston's second book, his first really original one; and it contained in addition to Judge Mike's story three other sketches: the already-printed Goosepond school tale along with "How Mr. Bill Williams Took the Responsibility" and "Miss Pea, Miss Spouter and the Yankee." Predictably, however, *Georgia Sketches* was not widely read. The national exposure that Johnston had experienced in *Porter's Spirit of the Times* in 1857 and that he had sought in an inquiry to *Harper's Magazine* in 1860 was simply not possible for a Southerner in the years 1861 to 1865.

Although Johnston could boast success in education at Rockby and literary triumph in Augusta, the Civil War did not allow much of the idyllic or the ideal for anyone, certainly not for a Southern planter who was a personal friend of Alexander H. Stephens, the Vice President of the Confederacy. Johnston had earlier noted the growth and foreseen the probable outcome of the antagonism between North and South. While before and during the war he each day hoped ardently for peace, he accurately predicted at the outset that it would be the bloodiest war of modern times. Although he had opposed secession, "in these troublous and perilous times," as he called them, he believed it was his duty to support Georgia and the new confederacy of which she was a part. How he was to do it was, however, another question, one that Johnston probably did not answer to the achievement of much peace of mind. He expected "of course" to go off to war, he wrote Alexander Stephens on May 21, 1861, despite what his family and personal affairs would suffer by his being away. He had thought much and seriously, he wrote Stephens, about "when men in my circumstances are thought to be needed." By September 1, 1861, he had decided he was needed more at home. Again, from Athens, he wrote to Stephens: "It is a dull, and seems to me a pitiful business to be teaching here when my friends are gone to war. I feel it is a misfortune that my domestic duties so despotically require me to stay at home. But when one's absence from home will do his family far more harm than his going to war will do his country good, even courage, courage of the best sort, requires him to stay."

These sentiments Johnston would self-consciously but probably more justifiably repeat to Stephens soon after going back to Hancock County. As the war and the increasing pressures of conscription wore on into September, 1862, Johnston wrote Judge James Thomas about getting a seat in the legislature and questioned Vice

President Stephens about appointment to some governmental post. Ultimately he was appointed to Governor Joseph E. Brown's staff as an aide-de-camp with some vague, undemanding responsibilities regarding the state militia. Brown, probably best remembered for his opposition to Confederate policies and especially conscription, provided exemptions from Confederate military service for large numbers of Georgians, who became known as "Joe Brown's Pets." Johnston's major service seems to have come in May, June, and July, 1864, when he stayed with and worked closely with Governor Brown in the vain effort to defend Atlanta. He ran perhaps his greatest risks after the war when he assisted his friends Robert Toombs and Alexander Stephens in projects of concealment and escape.

As Jimmy Ponder Voyles points out, Johnston in the *Autobiography* and in his fiction is "strangely reticent about the Civil War."[31] And for this silence Voyles offers some plausible reasons. Perhaps it was because of his personal opposition to secession. Perhaps, and this is very likely, it was his failure to be engaged in combat military service. Though semi-official as a result of the war, Johnston's colonelcy was still mostly honorary; William Tappan Thompson, another Georgia writer who had a gubernatorial aide-de-camp appointment initially, later assumed a regular combat commission. Certainly Johnston saw with sad dismay the effect of war upon combatants and noncombatants alike. The charitable and genteel qualities of the Southern people began to disappear before his eyes, and life on a Southern plantation, he said euphemistically, became "far less agreeable" after the close of "the Confederate war."

Truly now the world he loved was gone. Although after experiencing a serious drop-off in the last year of the war Rockby had rapidly regained capacity enrollment, the school and nothing else were quite the same economically or in any other way. Johnston seems honestly not to have been upset by the loss of his slaves. He says in his autobiography that he experienced "a sense of relief from very great responsibility" when emancipation became a fact; but apprehensive of the "deterioration of the white race in being thus surrounded by negroes," he was concerned about the assertive behavior of the new freedmen. Reconstruction life in Georgia was hard for such people as the Johnstons, and for them in particular it was made infinitely more difficult by the loss of fourteen-year-old Lucy Johnston on the last day of August, 1865. A beautiful, accomplished girl, she was a favorite of her father's, and he was prostrated by her death which, according to the obituary, followed a short and painful illness. That Mary Frances Johnston, as her husband noted often, never seemed very healthy living on a plantation seemed particularly ominous now.

A number of reasons, then, combined to make Johnston consider another move. Though he reports the outcome as a joint decision made "after much reflection," the idea of a removal from Georgia probably came from Mrs. Johnston, who then played an active part in finding a new home outside the South for her family. By June, 1867, with the help of friends in Baltimore, a promising location near that city had been secured. In July the family made its momentous move. The plan was to locate near a city so that Professor Johnston could establish a school and Mrs. Johnston conduct a market garden. "In addition to this," Johnston remarked significantly in a March 29, 1867, letter to Alexander Stephens, "I would like to be nearer where papers and magazines are published, believing I could do something by writing for them."

III   *The Sad and Serious Life of an Exile: The Maryland Years (1867 - 1898)*

The last thirty years of his life never brought Johnston again to residence in his beloved Georgia, but they did—partly for this very reason—bring what he had failed to achieve there: a full-time pursuit of letters and a literary reputation of national scope. The literary career was. necessitated by financial distress, however, and the reputation was ultimately as fleeting as its preparation had been long. The leading writers and critics of the nation gave him high praise and loyal friendships, but he said at last, "Life is so weary, I am glad to go." [32]

The Baltimore years can be divided into three fairly distinct periods. The first, during which Johnston tried with diminishing success to continue teaching and schoolkeeping, extended from 1867 to 1883. The climactic year of these sixteen was undoubtedly 1875, the year of his conversion to Roman Catholicism. The second period, during which Johnston devoted himself to writing, extended from 1883 to 1895. Then, from 1895 until his death in 1898 he was a government employee, working for most of this time in the Bureau of Education in Washington. In all three periods he lectured and wrote, for the first time receiving payment, but the Baltimore years neither began nor ended with these as his main pursuits. [33]

Leaving behind a thousand-acre estate whose value at one time approached $50,000, Johnston, with borrowed money, moved his family to nine acres of an attractive wooded estate known as "Chesnut Hill," located along the York road two or three miles north of Baltimore in the suburb of Waverly. The Johnstons had now eight children, ranging in age from twenty-two to just under two—three boys and five girls—Malcolm, Walton, Albon, Amy, Marianna, Richard, Ruth, and Effie. Their last child, Lucian, was born in Maryland in 1868. Using Rockby as a physical as well as an educational model, the Johnstons quickly prepared their new home for academic service. The new place and the new school they called "Pen Lucy," Johnston explaining that "pen" was Celtic for hill and "Lucy" was in memory of the dear, dark-haired girl whose grave they had deliberately but sadly left behind them in Georgia.

About forty boys, a capacity enrollment, followed Johnston from Georgia to continue their education at Pen Lucy beginning in September, 1867. A flyer for Pen Lucy indicates that it was indeed a continuation of Rockby, offering an essentially classical education with also rather unusual emphasis on music. Johnston made explicit claim in his prospectus that "pupils are treated, so far as practicable, as members of the family" and that "it is not a vain thing to expect and require even very young boys to understand, and appreciate, and practice the deportment of gentlemen."[34] Understanding and appreciating the need to cultivate a Maryland clientele, Johnston began immediate efforts toward this end by printing impressive testimonials from well-known men of Georgia. The proportion of day students gradually increased, but the school, said Johnston, "prospered as before." With her horticultural talents, Mrs. Johnston enhanced the beauty of a place already blessed by nature. Recalling the early pleasant, patriarchal life at Pen Lucy, some of the Johnston children remembered their father writing during the day on the shaded verandah or under the trees on the lawn and then wandering around the charming grounds at sunset, a shawl thrown around his shoulders, reciting Greek poetry.

Although he had difficulty in collecting the money due from the sale of Rockby, life generally went well for the Johnstons—and especially for the literary ambitions of the head of the household—for the first six or seven years at their new residence. In addition to being a center for fertilizer manufacture and distribution, Baltimore as a postwar haven for Southern expatriates also became an increasingly important cultural center. The Johnstons had a number of acquaintances already there, including such good old Hancock neighbors as the Edgar Dawsons and the Edgeworth Birds; and enhanced by memories of the Old South and by a love of literature and music, their circle of friends in Baltimore grew. Among the more significant friendships for Johnston were those with literary men, notably William Hand Browne, Lawrence Turnbull, Henry C. Turnbull, Jr., and Sidney Lanier. Johnston had apparently earlier written a series of humorous sketches for a Baltimore newspaper, but through Browne and the Turnbulls he gained acceptance for his work in a less transient periodical, *The New Eclectic*, later *The Southern Magazine*.

Johnston's first magazine publications in Baltimore (in *The Southern Review*) in 1868 and 1869 were essays, but in 1869, 1870, and 1871 *The New Eclectic* published the five of Johnston's tales and sketches that had been printed in Georgia plus three new ones. Later in 1871 all eight were collected and issued by Turnbull Brothers of Baltimore as *Dukesborough Tales* by Philemon Perch. A long story, "Old Friends and New," which appeared in *The Southern Magazine* in 1872, was added in 1874 to form a second edition of the title that would in time become Johnston's best-known one. In addition, Johnston collaborated with William Hand Browne to produce in 1872 an extensively enlarged edition of *The English Classics*—called now *English Literature: A Historical Sketch of English Literature From the Earliest Times*.

By 1873, Johnston might well have exclaimed, as Lanier soon would, that "the world has bloom'd again at Baltimore!" Well situated now, he returned to Georgia at least three times for pleasant visits, and in the summers of 1873 and 1874 he toured Europe, the first an all-expense-paid trip as a chaperone for one of his students and another youth. Although, as a student of English literature and history, Johnston must have enjoyed much of what he saw in Europe, he experienced more homesickness than anything else. And in 1873 he came home to a diminished enrollment at Pen Lucy, the beginning of a gradual ten-year decline which could not be halted short of the dissolution of the school and the end of Johnston's career as an educator. Because of falling cotton prices, Johnston had had apprehensions about the school from the beginning. Fairly successful attempts had been made to draw pupils from Baltimore and other more northern points, but the economic depression affecting Georgia at this time had a serious effect upon Pen Lucy, still heavily dependent upon fathers and sons of wealthy Georgia families. Only fourteen boys—six "in the house" and eight "outside"—were attending in the fall of 1874.

The shadowy handwriting on the wall in 1873 became clear script for the failure of Pen Lucy after 1875 when Johnston, following his wife's lead, was converted to the Roman Catholic faith. The conversion, when it became known, surprised and shocked many of Johnston's friends, especially those in Georgia. Historically, it is not quite so startling. Johnston had reacted strongly to religious intolerance and had done some reading and research in Catholicism as a result of the Know-Nothing campaign in Georgia in 1855. While he had declined the presidency of a denominational school, he had never relinquished a religious faith, had never failed for any length of time to worship publicly. Raised a Baptist, as a result of his father's conversion, he joined the Episcopal Church probably when he was in Athens; and though an Episcopalian he also attended Methodist services in Hancock, especially when his close friend and neighbor Bishop George F. Pierce was speaking. His correspondence over the years reveals that his religious beliefs were not merely public ones. As time passed, Johnston expressed a growing confidence in God and His providence, and the death of Lucy moved him to increased consideration of other-worldness and ultimately to a much deeper faith.

After the move to Maryland, the family became communicants of Saint John's Episcopal Church in Waverly, but by the fall of 1874 Mrs. Johnston had made a basic denominational change. Johnston himself read much about the Church for the next six months, and impressed by Newman's writings among others, made the decision to become a Roman Catholic in late June, 1875. Like Fanny, he received instructions from Father Dwight E. Lyman of Saint Mary's Catholic Church, Govans, and all of the Johnston children except the oldest three became one in this faith, Lucian much pleasing his parents by later becoming a priest. Though never as passionate in his religious beliefs as his wife, who was fanatical at times, Johnston became a devout Catholic and, in more ways than one, a valued spokesman for the Church. Writing to a cousin in Georgia in the early 1880s, he told of his change of faith, "of how surprised I have been not to have made it before, of how surprised I have been that any reasonable person should be any thing else than Catholic, of the incontrovertible claims the Catholic Church has to be the only Church of Christ, and of the ineffable consolation it has been to me in my thitherto vain endeavors to reconcile myself to the losses and the disharmonies of life, and my griefs in memory of my own numerous shortcomings in the attempted discharge of the various duties of my being."[35]

One of the most difficult of these duties at the time, as he also told a Georgia cousin, was the support of his family. Johnston evidently did not consider his Roman Catholicism one of his "shortcomings," but it was, as he knew, one reason for the diminishing patronage of his school and his diminishing income. Another reason which he would have recognized as a shortcoming was the rather heavy drinking in which there is reason to believe he indulged at this time. Johnston, to his wife's distaste, had always liked his toddies, but whether an increase in tippling was a cause or a result of the school's deterioration is difficult to say. Certainly Johnston faced penurious and trying times in the late 1870s and early 1880s, and when he was much worried about money, his disposition was sometimes not the sweetest. When it was no longer possible to board students at Pen Lucy, attempts were made, with many of the duties falling upon Amy Johnston, to conduct the school's classes over a grocery store at the corner of Maryland Avenue and North Avenue in Baltimore proper. For a while the family continued to live on the Waverly estate, but in 1883 the school had to be closed and Pen Lucy itself relinquished, and Johnston moved his family into the two floors, each consisting of only a single long room, over Cowman's grocery, Baltimore. In failing health herself, Amy attempted to supervise her two youngest sisters in teaching enough students to bring in a subsistence for the family.

"And then I bethought me to become an author," writes Johnston in his autobiography. He had, of course, been bethinking this for nearly thirty years, but with his teaching career all too clearly at an end, for the first time there was real promise of a career as a writer. Johnston's first remuneration for a story had come in the desperate times of the late 1870s and as the result of a friendship that had much helped in other ways to make this period bearable. Johnston had probably met Sidney Lanier soon after Lanier arrived in Baltimore in 1873, and the two men and their families eventually became very close, at no time more so than in 1877 and 1878 when the Laniers lived on Denmead Street and Lanier taught mathematics part time at Johnston's school. "My dear Colonel," Lanier once wrote, "(but why should I not spell it Kernel,—as being one to whom other men are but shells or husks?)."[36] To his nostalgic, story-writing friend, Lanier brought the sympathetic knowledge, critical perception, and national publishing connections that Johnston needed so much at this time, and it was due to Lanier's knowledgeable tutoring and subsequent recommendation that a rather surprised Johnston was first paid for a story, "Mr. Neelus Peeler's Conditions," which appeared in *Scribner's Monthly Magazine* in June, 1879. Six other stories followed in *Scribner's* and *Harper's New Monthly Magazine* in 1881 and 1882, and when in 1883 Harper & Brothers issued these seven and the nine previously published stories in a new *Dukesborough Tales*, Richard Malcolm Johnston found himself a national literary figure at the age of sixty-one.

What remained of his life was, naturally, much more public than what had preceded, and these fifteen years, 1883 to 1898, provide the picture of Johnston that has endured, rather as if, in defiance of the universal scheme, his youth and middle age had never existed. They were prolific and active years until almost the very end. The *Life of Alexander H. Stephens* by Johnston and Browne, first published in 1878, was issued in a new and revised edition after Stephens's death in 1883, and a travel book called *Two Gray Tourists* appeared in 1885. For the most part, however, Johnston for eleven or twelve years after 1883 poured his energies into the creation of stories about Middle Georgia. Not quite so ingenuous as he is usually pictured, he wrote to such established literary figures as Frank Stockton, Charles Dudley Warner, and Edgar W. Nye, and he followed their advice of first publishing his stories in the magazines and then collecting them into books. Although such collections never sold very well, this method enabled him to get as much fiscal mileage out of his efforts as possible. Collections appeared in 1888, 1891, two in 1892, 1894, and 1897, these in addition to yet another but reworked and abbreviated *Dukesborough Tales* in 1892 and four novels or novellettes, two of which had previously appeared in magazines: *Old Mark Langston* (1884), *Ogeechee Cross-Firings* (1889), *Widow Guthrie* (1890), and *Pearce Amerson's Will* (1898). The raw material for them all was the same. He had written earlier, Johnston reports in the *Autobiography*, "stories intended to illustrate characters and scenes among the simple rural folk of my native region as they were during the period of my childhood, before the age of railroads. To this period I have always recurred, and I do so now, with much fondness, and indeed with high admiration for the good sense, the simplicity, the uprightness, the loyalty to every known duty that characterized the rural people of middle Georgia."

Although, appropriately, it is for his local-color fiction that he is remembered, the writing and marketing of this work comprised only part of the literary activity into which Johnston threw himself during these years, his financial precariousness still far from being over. Public lectures on literature, with which he had made a start in a series for the Peabody Institute in 1870, were continued at an accelerated pace. A series by Professor R. M. Johnston became practically an annual event at the convent of Notre Dame in Baltimore during the 1880s, for example. In the 1890s he was a regular and popular lecturer at sessions of the Catholic Summer School, appearing most often in Plattsburgh, New York, but going also to New London, Connecticut, and Madison, Wisconsin. Some of these presentations were published as part of the Catholic Summer and Winter School Library in 1897 in a volume entitled *Lectures on Literature: English, French and Spanish.* Many other literary and historical essays were written expressly for publication—some as hackwork, a number of others for Catholic periodicals. Two collections of lectures and articles—and Johnston hoped to do more—were published as *Studies, Literary and Social,* First and Second Series, in 1891 and 1892.

Having made a regular feature of reading aloud from literary works to his students and long having had reputation in Georgia as an entertaining raconteur, Johnston added readings from "original sources" to his scholarly lecture series in the early 1880s. Soon thereafter, having gained something of a reputation as a writer, he began to make separate public appearances reading from his own works, his favorite platform piece being "The Early Majority of Mr. Thomas Watts." Still returning to Georgia for early summer visits as often as he could, Johnston gave readings at many towns and cities in his native state, and he traveled to New Orleans, Nashville, Birmingham, Indianapolis, Chicago, and various northeastern locations for reading appearances. Probably his most memorable reading was given on January 17, 1889, when Mark Twain, filling in for Thomas Nelson Page as a personal favor to Johnston, traveled down to Baltimore to appear with him—and, so the story goes, to donate to him all of the proceeds. Twain, Johnston, and other notables also gave special readings and participated in special lobbying efforts for the American Copyright League. In addition, Johnston made a number of other public presentations which, though not readings from his works, were nostalgic factual revelations of the bases of his fiction. In the 1890s he spoke by invitation, for example, before the Southern Historical Association, the Twentieth Century Club of Chicago, and the New England Society of New York City.

Though he was now, as he rather often reminded some of his influential literary correspondents, an old man who still had to work very hard, the later years of his life must have brought much satisfaction to Johnston. He had never become the poet he obviously and even desperately wanted to be. He had not written the successful plays—one was attempted with Joel Chandler Harris—that he had hoped to write. But surely the fame he belatedly achieved on the crest of the wave of local-color fiction exceeded the expectations and indeed the dreams of that malcontent young lawyer in Georgia in the 1850s. When the Catholic Association of Baltimore hosted a grand Golden Wedding Reception for Mr. and Mrs. Johnston in 1894, testimonies and praise poured in from practically every important literary figure in the country. Some of these men and women were only acquaintances, but a great many were genuine personal friends. In 1895 his valued local friends at the University Club in Baltimore purchased a portrait of him by Thomas C. Corner to be hung in a place of honor at the Club, and three institutions of higher learning in three different states made him, twice in 1895 and once again in 1897, a Doctor of Laws.

Serious critics of his literary works have invariably noted Johnston's narrowness of range, and it is to his credit that, in the midst of tributes and honorings, he also knew, and knew it was time to cease mining a vein that had perhaps been mined too long already. In 1894 the "dereliction of understanding and invention" which he knew would come had not yet come, and realizing that the proceeds from his writing were getting smaller, he began looking for another means of livelihood. "I did not like the idea of continuing at story telling down to the very grave," he explains in his autobiography, an explanation and an attitude that he had expressed more affectingly as early as 1888 to E. C. Stedman, then a literary critic of some influence. "Somehow," he wrote Stedman on September 14, 1888, "I dont quite like the idea of going out of the world known to it only as an aged clown, particularly for that during all my time since my boyhood my life has been a serious, if not a sad one."[37] With the same point and the same reference to "a clown—a circus clown," he wrote to Stedman in 1894 saying that he felt "the need of some change of work in what little time is left me" and asking Stedman's aid in helping him secure what he had referred to in an earlier letter as "a little corner in Washington."[38] Johnston's solicitations of Stedman and others gained him in March of 1895 a position in the U.S. Department of Labor, from which after work on two different projects, some objections from the Civil Service Commissioner, and two months' unemployment, he "got into" the Bureau of Education as "Confidential Secretary" to the Commissioner at an annual salary of $1200.[39] For the next year and a half, commuting by train each day from Baltimore, he faithfully fulfilled the assignments of his "public service" here, including the pleasant and familiar task of writing about early educational life in Middle Georgia.

In ceasing to be a professional storyteller Johnston felt that he had applied the counsel in Philip James Bailey's *Festus*, "Know when to die." From at least the time he had suggested it as a debate topic to bewildered Rockby students and increasingly as he passed through the 1890s, this admonition was much in his mind. He spoke often of his old age to his new literary friends and correspondents, remarking once to E. C. Stedman that he sometimes seemed "to myself to have lived from the beginning of time."[40] He was much affected by the death of his wife in February, 1897, and close friends marked a decline in his own health and spirits from this point. Writing to his daughter Effie in the spring of 1897, he talked of his anxiousness to be "home," told of unsuccessful attempts to repurchase Pen Lucy, and reported to her his increasing preference for solitude.[41] He became ill in May, 1898, and was soon confined to his room under the care of his daughters and a trained nurse. In August, at his request, he was moved to a Baltimore hospital, where on September 23, 1898, he died peacefully of old age. Funeral services were held in the Saint Ignatius Catholic Church of Baltimore, and Johnston's body, dressed in the white habit of the Third Order of Saint Dominic, was laid to rest beside his wife's in the churchyard of Saint Mary's Church in Govanstown.

As soon as he heard the news, George Washington Cable wrote to Miss Ruth Johnston. "Your father," he said, "was a man whom no one knew without feeling for him a tender and deep-seated affection. He made the world happier daily and hourly by the noble sweetness of his personality no less than by the purity and kind cheer and humor of his masterful stories."[42]

CHAPTER 2

Dukesborough Tales

I F Richard Malcolm Johnston is remembered, it is likely to be for his *Dukesborough Tales*. Less likely to be recalled is that this title made four separate appearances, no two of the exactly named collections being exactly the same. And, even before the first of these appearances in 1871, four "Dukesborough tales" had been collected as *Georgia Sketches* (1864). The history of Walt Whitman's *Leaves of Grass* may provide something of a parallel, but few books or titles have had such a strange publication history as that of Johnston's best-known work—if indeed it can be called a single work and not simply a series of gatherings together of what at various times seemed profitably gatherable.

Informed, scholarly considerations of Richard Malcolm Johnston have come to include several common observations or assessments regarding *Dukesborough Tales*. The first is that it was this work—the 1883 version specifically—that focused national attention upon Johnston. And from a knowledge of American literary history, of the successive national thirsts for various local colors, comes the explanation that this triumph was largely because of tales about the right place appearing at the right time. Neither the pre- nor the post-1883 editions of *Dukesborough Tales* had nearly so great an impact.

Next, and more critically, the tales and sketches published under this title are regarded as "typical" and seen generally as the "best" of Johnston's literary works. They are typical in type (shorter prose tales and sketches) and in subject (the middle-class white people of Middle Georgia in the 1820s, '30s, and '40s). Also, because several undergo successive, rather extensive revision for their several appearances, they evidence a typicality of treatment or style which is at once both personal and historical.

The unusual historical perspective that an inclusive consideration of *Dukesborough Tales* can provide is what allows Johnston to be seen as a link between the humorists of the Old Southwest and the later local colorists of the South, the Old Southwest writers now generally being appraised more highly. Thus, Johnston's "evolution" sacrificed essential vitality for polish and formula. What he gained in narrative tightness, he lost in strength and originality of characterization, which was and remains his real strength. Containing, then, his earliest work, though sometimes in altered form, *Dukesborough Tales* retains a freshness and a spontaneity that was lamentably uncapturable in the coils of later nineteenth-century publication.

I *Who, What, When, Where, Why, and How*

"In making up a story of imagination I could never do without places," wrote Johnston in his autobiography, and *Dukesborough Tales* is proof of the accuracy of his self-knowledge. "I must," he went on, "see in my mind those places I have seen with my eyes." And "of all places," the village of Powelton, Georgia, "has been ever most fondly loved by me . . . ." And then specifically: "by the name 'Dukesborough' was intended Powelton . . . ." The name, Johnston claimed, was "entirely arbitrary," but like the discoverers of real gold in Georgia in the nineteenth century, he staked a successful claim beside Duke's Creek.

If not quite so hard to discover, an outline of the public life of the Dukesborough tales is about as bewildering as an outline of Johnston's professional life during the 1840s and '50s. Although he had the recording of a local history in mind from the beginning of his story writing and had in fact already made his choice of the name of "Dukesborough," the first collection of Johnston's tales did not advertise so specific a locale. *Georgia Sketches*, "From Recollections of an Old Man" by Philemon Perch, has usually been seen as obviously and even opportunistically in the tradition of A. B. Longstreet's famous *Georgia Scenes* (1835). Published in 1864 in Augusta, *Georgia Sketches* managed to get together—though in different-sized print and paper—four tales that were to be the foundation of the later Dukesborough collections.

First was "Five Chapters of a History" which had appeared in *Porter's Spirit of the Times* in December, 1857, and which had then been reprinted in Georgia newspapers and periodicals—the Augusta *Constitutionalist* and the *Georgia Literary and Temperance Crusader*, for example. Rechristened "Mr. Israel Meadows and His

School" in *Georgia Sketches*, it would undergo yet another change
of name in 1869 to "The Goosepond School." "Five Chapters of a
History: A Georgia Court, Forty Years Ago," which had appeared in
Southern Field and Fireside in January, 1863, appeared under the
name "Judge Mike and His Court," a title to be altered only slightly later to "Judge Mike's Court." The other two sketches were here
printed for the first time. "How [Mr.] Bill Williams Took the
Responsibility" reintroduced Johnston's favorite subject of school
life and introduced a man who would become one of his favorite
characters, while "Miss Pea, Miss Spouter and the Yankee," later to
be renamed "The Pursuit of Mr. Adiel Slack," utilized a favorite
subject and situation of Old Southwestern humor. As a matter of
fact, the running title of *Georgia Sketches* is "Humorous Tales."

Although it was later to appear in *Dukesborough Tales*, a fifth
story called "The Last Day of Mr. Williamson Slippey, Salt
Merchant" (later, simply "Mr. Williamson Slippey and His Salt")
which had been published in the March 28, 1863, number of
Southern Field and Fireside was not collected in *Georgia Sketches*.
The reason was perhaps its Civil War topic. At any rate, with five
published stories to his pseudonymous but hardly anonymous credit
before 1865, R. M. Johnston was two or three off the mark when he
so modestly later claimed that he had written only "two or three"
stories before he left Georgia. He had tried futilely just before he
left, in fact, to interest some Northern publishers in these productions.

The four collected Georgia sketches, said Philemon Perch, were
written for "the entertainment there was in thus employing" some
of his leisure time. Phil's creator had him make the same prefatory
explanation for *Dukesborough Tales*, but the creator later explained
autobiographically that writing such tales in Baltimore had been
undertaken for "subduing as far as possible the sense of
homesickness" and for "alleviating the burden of misapprehension
which soon befell me" after removal from Georgia. Literary acquaintances had also befallen him, and from November, 1869,
through October, 1870, Johnston was absent from the pages of
Baltimore's *The New Eclectic Magazine* only in the August and
September numbers. All five of his previously published but now
reworked and retitled Georgia tales appeared, to which were added
in June and July two new sketches: "The Early Majority of Mr.
Thomas Watts" and "The Organ-Grinder." And in the summer of
1871 "Investigations Concerning Mr. Jonas Lively" was published
in *The New Eclectic's* successor, *The Southern Magazine*.

Drawn from and "dedicated to memories of the old times, the grim and rude but hearty old times in Georgia," these were the eight sketches that, according to Mr. Perch, he was now venturing to call tales and that he had been persuaded, "perhaps too easily," to allow to "be published in a little book." [1] This collection was the first edition of *Dukesborough Tales,* published late in 1871 by Turnbull Brothers of Baltimore and, if the golden signature on the cover were to be believed, written by Philemon Perch. Three years later Turnbull and Perch brought out what was called a second and enlarged edition, the enlargement consisting of the tacking on of "Old Friends and New," a long piece that had already been labeled as Dukesborough tale number nine in its appearance in *The Southern Magazine* from February through August, 1872.

Both of the Baltimore-published *Dukesborough Tales* are today considered rare books. Second-edition copies are scarcer than those of the first, and copies of the third appearance of the title, which was New York-issued but in a newspaper-like format, are rarer still. In 1874 Johnston, though author of eight individual tales and three separate collections of works drawn "mostly from imagination," had yet to receive any pecuniary compensation for his "essays on that line of endeavor." But with the interest of such national publishers as Harper's and Scribner's, Philemon Perch would soon be able to open a small bank account.

On January 12, 1883, Harper & Brothers brought out as No. 290 in its paperback Franklin Square Library a collection of sixteen stories entitled *Dukesborough Tales.* For the first time Johnston's own name was affixed to a collection of his "mostly" imaginative work. "The first nine of the following sketches," he explained in the foreword, "were announced as coming from Mr. Philemon Perch, fond and garrulous from advanced age, contemporary with the characters, and an actor in some of the scenes described. On the production of 'Mr. Neelus Peeler's Conditions,' the author acting upon the advice of friends, dropped this *nom de plume*, and thereafter appended his proper signature." Thus, in a twenty-five cent ephemeral edition but at last available to a national audience, all nine constituents of the 1874 edition of *Dukesborough Tales* were republished and recollected, and seven new tales which had since been published were collected for the first time. The pages of *Scribner's Monthly* had originally contained the first two of the latter: "Mr. Neelus Peeler's Conditions" (June, 1879) and "The Expensive Treat of Colonel Moses Grice" (January, 1881). The remaining five had all appeared in *Harper's New Monthly*

Magazine: "Puss Tanner's Defence" (February, 1881), "The [Unexpected Parting of the] Beazley Twins" (May, 1881), "The Various Languages of Billy Moon" (August, 1881), "The Jonce Trammel Compromise" (January, 1882), and "King William and His Armies" (June, 1882).

This lineup of 1883 constituted what nine years later Johnston was misleadingly to refer to as "the original sixteen" Dukesborough tales. The occasion for his comment was the preface to the fourth and last appearance of a collection under this name, *Dukesborough Tales: The Chronicles of Mr. Bill Williams* published by D. Appleton and Company in its Town and Country Library in 1892. "By friends and many acquaintances," Johnston said, he had "been often advised to re-publish *Dukesborough Tales* in a form more convenient than that in which it was first issued [evidently, and again misleadingly, the 1883 version]." "Acting upon this counsel," he chose and "carefully revised" six stories which "relate mainly to incidents in the career of Mr. Bill Williams and his nearest associates." Headed by the doubly Georgian "The Goosepond School" and "How Mr. Bill Williams Took the Responsibility," the remaining selections were "Investigations Concerning Mr. Jonas Lively," "Old Friends and New," "The Expensive Treat of Colonel Moses Grice," and "King William and His Armies."

To bring these to publication again had taken some negotiation, and Johnston, most hopeful of further new Dukesborough reissues, was not very much pleased with Appleton's behavior after the book was out. In his hours of truth, though, he should have recognized that *Dukesborough Tales* was like the decayed and deserted village of Dukesborough to which he had given a reflective sigh in the later-appended first section of "The Goosepond School." All places have their times to fall, he realized, just as all people have their times to die:

> . . . my position about Dukesborough is, that it had lived out its life. It had run its race, like all other things, places, and persons that have lived out their lives and run their races; and when that was done, Dukesborough *had* to fall. It had not lived very long, and it had run but slowly, if indeed, it can be said to have run at all. But it reached its journey's end.[2]

He had not gotten much money, but Johnston had in fact gotten a great deal of mileage out of *Dukesborough Tales.*

II   "*Taking the Census*"

If Thomas Nelson Page is to be given credit for preserving the aristocratic regime of the South, says Ima Honaker Herron, R. M. Johnston "deserves recognition as a recorder of a life equally as significant in the South, the ante-bellum rural community and small town of Middle Georgia."[3] "I doubt," said an earlier and even more appreciative commentator on Dukesborough, "if there is another village in America that has had its home life so graphically portrayed or its private history so fully narrated. . . ."[4] The evidence or reasons for such statements extend beyond *Dukesborough Tales*, but here, necessarily, is where they begin.

Dukesborough, through a single-minded use of this setting, became truly "our town" to thousands of intrigued American readers in the 1880s and 1890s. Johnston's was indeed "the story of a country town," but unlike Edgar Watson Howe's novel of this title (1883), it was a story fleshed out from many short stories with a common setting and with some common characters and vivified by a sense of nostalgic, loving proprietorship[5] very different from the despair and desolation of Howe's work.

The title of another, less well known story of rural America offers nearly the perfect entree to consideration of Johnston's tales of Dukesborough: Johnson Jones Hooper's "Taking the Census" (1843). This title is suggestive for Johnston, for as the titles of his own works reveal, people are what is supremely important. Plots are weak, and even incident is secondary to and dependent upon personality. Johnston pictured in detail practically every major social institution of the time and place, and he paused more than once to draw with care the physical setting, even to locating the various domiciles of Dukesborough. But it was and is his characters who give meaning and definition to event and setting; it is they who give life to his literature, and it is with these individuals that Johnston has some chance of enduring through his literary works.

Philemon Perch and his older but admiring friend "Mr. Bill" Williams are recurrent and therefore prominent persons in *Dukesborough Tales*, often figuring in Johnston's narrative machinery. Despite—or perhaps because of—their longevity, they are not, however, the vividly memorable characters he was sometimes able to achieve in the sharp, quick strokes of single portraiture. It is precisely this achievement that marks and makes the best of the *Dukesborough Tales:* "The Goosepond School," "How Mr. Bill Williams Took the Responsibility," "Investigations Concerning Mr. Jonas Lively," "The Expensive Treat of Colonel Moses Grice," "The Various Languages of Billy Moon," and "The Early Majority of Mr. Thomas Watts."

Probably, as Johnston recalled, there was no subject to which his old-time lawyer friends and colleagues recurred more often and more fondly than their schooldays, this despite the sometimes cruel masters and primitive principles that had obtained in the old-field schools, so called because they were built in no longer cultivated fields of Southern plantations. Ninety-one of his fictional Middle Georgians are either students or teachers,[6] and Johnston's deep interest and concern with education are, of course, manifest in his own long and reformistic pedagogical life. His major achievement is sometimes said to be the faithful record of the early educational life of his native region. His best-known story is almost surely "The Goosepond School," and Israel Meadows in this first of all the tales endures as Johnston's most memorable creation.

Revealing much about early nineteenth-century school practices, "The Goosepond School" relates the unpremeditated physical overthrow of a sadistic Georgia schoolmaster. Seen as Johnston increasingly forced his readers to see it, the story is one of rightful revolution in which goodness and innocence gain their inevitable triumph over despotism. Like John Milton, Johnston may be charged, however, with drawing his avatar of evil if not more attractive, then certainly larger and more impressive than his paragon of good. Israel Meadows, though soundly thrashed and thoroughly humiliated by Brinkly Glisson within the narrative, reigns sovereign once more after narrative and commentary's close. Johnston knew about a flogging deserter from the British navy who had kept school around the end of the eighteenth century in the Goosepond neighborhood along the Broad River in Oglethorpe County, Georgia. He had heard friends, and especially Alexander Stephens, talk of raw schoolmasters and student rebellion. And from Messrs. Hogg, Yellowby, and Hilsman, his own teachers, he knew personally of pedagogical irrationality and punishments and remembered at least one forcible "turn-out" and "ducking" of a teacher by students. The bastard master of his fictional Goosepond school is perhaps all of these, but he assuredly is more.

Mr. "Iserl" Meadows, says Johnston,

was a man thirty-five or forty years of age, five feet ten inches in height, with a lean figure, dark complexion, very black and shaggy hair and eyebrows, and a grim expression of countenance. The occupation of training the youthful mind and leading it to the fountains of wisdom, as delightful and interesting as it is, was not, in fact, Mr. Meadows' choice when, on arriving at manhood's estate, he looked about him for a career in which he might the most surely develop and advance his being in life. Indeed, those who had been the witnesses of his youth and young manhood, and of the opportunities which he had been favored withal for getting instruction for himself, were no little surprised when they heard that in the county of Hancock their old acquaintance was in the actual prosecution of the profession of schoolmaster. . . . But Mr. Israel Meadows, although not a man of great learning, was a great way removed from being a fool. He had a considerable amount of the wisdom of this world which comes to a man from other sources besides books. He was like many other men in one respect. He was not to be restrained from taking office by the consciousness of attainments inadequate to the discharge of its duties. This is a species of indelicacy which, of all others, is attended by fewest practical results. (pp. 11, 14)

Never having been a pupil himself, Israel Meadows had become a teacher only after the illegal sources of his family's lucrative corn-supplying business had come to undeniable light. (His father's identity had never come to any kind of light.) Being thus rapidly transformed from violator to maker of laws and from escaper to administrator of punishment, he entered upon these aspects of his new vocation with assiduous vengeance and secure delight. Neither delight nor security could his scholars have, who were punished first and then informed of the newly formulated offense; but vengeance for them all came one November day by the hands and literally the fists of fifteen-year-old Brinkly Glisson. The conscientious but, by Mr. Meadows, much-abused son of a widow, Brinkly took all he could take of Meadows's "imposin' disposition" and painful, humiliating discipline. Having again watched his classmates suffer in the sadistic hickory-switching games of "circus" and "horsin'," he issued a pleading warning to Mr. Meadows about his own individual flogging, and when this warning was ignored, "the long-pent-up resentment of his soul gushed forth, and the fury of a demon glared from his eyes." In the wrestling, tumbling, gourging, hair-pulling, fist-throwing fracas that followed, Brinkly finally made Mr. Meadows beg for mercy. Allen Thigpen, an older pupil who had learned of the schoolmaster's sordid history, pronounced the benediction and issued the threat that hurried the battered Meadows out of the district.

The controlling authorial presence which is evident in the description of Meadows quoted above characterizes the whole of "The Goosepond School," as it does all of Johnston's tales. The long tongue-in-cheek account of Israel's prior fortunes and misfortunes firmly establishes that appealing rascal's character, setting a tone and providing a humorous bias which sadism and a little bloodshed can not later vitiate. Johnston enters into, for him, some unusual speculation about Mr. Meadows's motives, but while all of the events and descriptions of the tale clearly emerge from an audience-conscious raconteur, Meadows is allowed at least some little self-dramatization—nowhere better, probably, than in his baiting of the students and in his careful little manipulations to avoid confrontation with hefty eighteen-year-old Allen Thigpen.

Just as the humorous, satirical interpretation of Meadows's earlier history is an enjoyment, authorial selection of detail is a granted prerogative and often a commendably exercised one. Little Asa Boatright's scheme of marking and learning only every fourth word for his spelling lesson, the once shocked but then recovered students entering upon an elaborate mimicry of the past regime after Meadows's departure, Meadows's timid and rather sad attempt to shake hands with Allen Thigpen as he leaves, his rageful but impotent shaking of both his hands at the distant schoolhouse after he has left: these are, for example, fine little realistic touches. But less agreeable and grantable, more like heavy-handed blows to modern sensibility, are the obtrusive expressions of righteous partisanship and blatant didactic commentary to which Johnston subjects the reader in all except the very first versions of this story. If the height of authorial commentary and moral flight are reached at the end of the tale, here also are the depths of bathos after Mrs. Glisson has learned of events at the school:

"Glory! glory! hallelujah!" shouted again and sung the mother.
Let her shout and sing. Sing away and shout, thou bereaved, at this one little triumph of thine only beloved! Infinite Justice! pardon her for singing and shouting now, when her only child, though poor and an orphan, though bruised and torn, seems to her overflowing eyes grand and beautiful, as if he were a royal hero's son, and the inheritor of his crown. (p. 45)

It was, thus, not a qualitative gain when "Five Chapters of a History" was expanded to eight chapters of moral sentimentality. Fortunately, some admirable dashes of local color remain, however, and so does, uniquely, Mr. Israel Meadows, larger than ever by contrast.

"How Mr. Bill Williams Took the Responsibility" is the story that introduced this favored title character, who was ultimately to appear in seven of Johnston's tales. Like only "The Goosepond School" besides, this story appeared in every "Dukesborough" collection from *Georgia Sketches* through the final 1892 version, which, significantly, was subtitled "The Chronicles of Mr. Bill Williams." Also like "The Goosepond School," what this tale most memorably chronicles is the deserved embarrassing predicament of a cowardly, tyrannical old-field schoolmaster.

Josiah Lorriby is the name of the person—Occupation: Pedagogue—whom this story contributes to the vital statistics of the census of Dukesborough. The whole Lorriby household may well, as a matter of fanciful fact, deserve such note; certainly, to little Philemon Perch, they were impossible not to notice:

> Mr. Josiah Lorriby was a remarkable man, at least in appearance. He was below the middle height, but squarely built. His body was good enough, but his other parts were defective. He had a low flat head, with very short hair and very long ears. His arms were reasonably long, but his hands and legs were disproportionately short. Many tales were told of his feet, on which he wore shoes with iron soles. He was sitting on a split-bottom chair, on one side of the fire-place. Under him, with his head peering out between the rounds, sitting on his hind legs and standing on his fore legs, was a small yellow dog, without tail or ears. The dog's name was Rum. On the other side of the hearth, in another split-bottom, sat a tall, raw-boned woman with the reddest eyes that I have ever seen. This was Mrs. Mehitable, Mr. Lorriby's wife. She had ridden to the school on a small, aged mare, perfectly white and totally blind. Her name was Kate.
>
> When I had surveyed these four personages—this satyr of a man, this tailless dog, this red-eyed woman, and this blind old mare, a sense of fear and helplessness came over me, such as I had never felt before, and have never felt since. . . .[7]

Mr. Lorriby was not, the narrator carefully states, the *knock down and drag out* type of schoolmaster "such . . . as Israel Meadows." But like Meadows, Mr. Lorriby was spineless and principleless, and once he learned the prejudices of the community about whipping (no lickin', no larnin'), he set about his flogging duties with all the vigor and unaccountability of ol' Israel. He did sometimes give boys the opportunity foolishly or chivalrously to take a girl's punishment for her,

but even so he made his way floggingly through the whole school pop-
ulation except for two imposingly big boys, Bill Williams and
Jeremiah Hobbes, and one girl, Betsy Ann Acry, the "plump,
delicious-looking" "belle of the school." The day came, however,
when Betsy Ann, disliked by the husband-dominating Mrs. Lorriby,
had to be called to task. To save her from punishment was, of course,
the responsibility that the admiring Bill Williams took, and this taking
presented a crisis of immense proportions for Mr. Lorriby. Seeking
refuge behind his wife when it appeared that Bill might be the giver
rather than receiver of blows, the schoolmaster was "more than
satisfied" when Bill, soon to enter upon the prestigious position of a
clerkship in Dukesborough, finally offered to take the punishment for
Betsy Ann. The long-suffering school children felt betrayed, but Mr.
Lorriby, in a paroxysm of relief, declined to administer the flogging
and delivered instead a marvelously revealing and utterly incom-
prehensible oration:

> "I am proud this day of William Williams. It air so, and I can but say I am
> proud of him. William Williams were now in a position to stand up and shine
> in his new spere of action. If he went to Dukesborough to keep store thar, he
> mout now go sayin' that as he had been a good scholar, so he mout expect to be
> a good clerk, and fit to be trusted, yea, with thousands upon thousands, ef sich
> mout be the case. But as it was so, and as he have been to us all as it war, and no
> difficulties, and no nuthin' of the sort, and he war goin', and it mout be soon,
> yea, it mout be to-morrow, from this school straight intoo a store, I cannot, nor
> I cannot. No, far be it. This were a skene too solemn and too lovely for sich. I
> cannot, nor I cannot. William Williams may now take his seat." (pp. 72 - 73)

Ostensibly telling the story in his old age, Philemon Perch was a
youthful participant and witness of the scenes he narrates in "How
Mr. Bill Williams Took the Responsibility." Johnston says in the
Autobiography that he "recalled" one of his own teachers, Josiah
Yellowby, and Yellowby's wife, Delilah, and indeed the Yellowby
menagerie, Rum and Kate, in drawing the Lorriby family portrait.
The idea of little Phil's being put under the care of and riding to
school on the shoulders of neighborly big Bill Williams emerges from
the experience of little Alexander H. Stephens. The added interest
contributed by Phil and Mr. Bill does not, however, add much to the
literary value of this tale. It, like "The Goosepond School," is
rendered anticlimactic by an explanatory focus on the nominal hero at
the end, and again the reader is treated to auctorial disquisition, this
time on educational conditions and attitudes. Not very organic, such
narrative inclusions as the relationship of the incipient revolutionary

Seaborn Byne with his little brother Joel and the molasses incident involving Phil and Martin Granger seem valid but ill-proportioned attempts at realism and local color. Getting surely some feel for school life in "the grim and rude but hearty old times," the reader is, nevertheless, grasped firmly only by Josiah Lorriby—with, of course, the assistance of his fiery red-eyed wife. The satirical preliminary overview is absent, and so, more than with Israel Meadows, Lorriby's character emerges from an immediate perspective and from the action of the tale itself.

The character of Mr. Jonas Lively also emerges from an immediate, participatory perspective and through the agencies of Phil Perch and Bill Williams, although in this case Phil is relating what Mr. Bill has related to him. Israel Meadows, Josiah Lorriby, and Jonas Lively are all "originals," as Henry M. Alden admiringly called the *Dukesborough* characters of Johnston, himself an "original" as a storyteller, according to Alden. But though Israel and Josiah are well individualized, Johnston's two schoolmasters are, unfortunately, all too representative of the pedagogues of that time; indeed, although the works themselves seem ample contradiction, it has been suggested that Johnston wrote these school sketches as propaganda for educational reform. Representative of no group or type—his occupation is one of the things needing "investigating"—Jonas Lively is, however, about as unique and original as an "original" can be. He is so, that is, in the 1871 and 1874 editions, but appreciably less so in later versions.

Set after Mr. Bill Williams has become established at Bland and Jones's store in Dukesborough and has advertised himself as an expert on all persons in and about the community, "Investigations Concerning Mr. Jonas Lively" reports the findings of the curious and petty-proud clerk whose record of absolute gossipy intelligence is marred by the enigmatic Lively. Mr. Lively, somewhere in his fifties, was "a remarkably silent man" who had been living for two or three years at the Hodge place about a mile outside town; more precisely, he boarded now with the widowed Melvina Hodge and Susan Temple, a poor orphaned relation who had earlier been taken into the household by Mr. Hodge. Although he did a little horse doctoring and made occasional speculative purchases, Lively did not seem to have "any regular business." Most curiously, he never took off his hat. He was in appearance

. . . quite stout in body, but of moderate-sized legs. He had a brown complexion, brown hair, and black eyebrows. His eyes were a mild green, with some tinge of red in the whites. His nose was Roman, or would have been if it had been longer; for just as it began to hook and become Roman it stopped short, as if upon reflection it thought it wrong to ape ancient and especially foreign manners. He always wore a long black frock-coat, either gray or black trousers and vest, and a very stout, low-crowned furred hat. He carried a hickory walking-stick with a hooked handle. (pp. 79 - 80)

The really interesting and original things about Mr. Lively are discovered by Bill Williams on a trumped-up stay at "Cousin Malviny" Hodge's when he spies on Mr. Lively at bedtime from outside that gentleman's bedroom window. Most important to Mr. Bill, he learns that Jonas Lively wears a wig, but he also witnesses Jonas's pipe-smoking and other pre-retirement rituals and learns his secret of certain adjustments and turnings-inside-out of his clothes that give him several outfits all in one. This latter trick, incidentally, is one in which Johnston himself engaged according to one of his New York editor friends, and it is a procedure F. Hopkinson Smith attributes to his lovable old Colonel Carter of Cartersville, supposedly modeled on Johnston. Reminiscent of Poe's "The Man Who Was All Used Up," the whole peeping episode—the basic situation, the disclosures, the mode of making the disclosures—is even more remindful of George Washington Harris's Sut Lovingood yarns. Whatever may have been Johnston's own associations with this part of the tale, however, his evaluation of it was low, and calling Bill's account of Jonas's "carrins on" too circumstantial and prolonged, he whacked off four delightful and telling pages for the 1883 and 1892 editions.

Just as Jonas Lively is best revealed in earlier versions of *Dukesborough Tales,* he is essentially revealed early in a story which goes on and on without significantly adding to his characterization. As almost all commentators on "Investigations" have observed, what Johnston has here is essentially two stories: one, Mr. Bill Williams's questionably attained personal discoveries about Mr. Lively; and second, a story of courtship and marriage involving the discovery of a lost will and having a surprise ending (Mr. Lively marries Susan Temple after Mrs. Hodge has thrown her matrimonial net out for him). Bill Williams is allowed to relate from his personal experience the humorous sequence of events at the Hodge place when the newlyweds return, and he does gain a little more knowledge about Mr. Lively's past which he can add at this point. In the meantime, however, Philemon Perch has come in with omniscient knowledge and as authoritative commentator to discuss Mrs. Hodge's "antecedents," in particular the wonderful transformations and effects of a woman in search of a husband. Like the amused and amusing discussion of Israel Meadows's antecedents, this portion is entertainingly characteristic of Johnston's humor, but it is here a contributing part of an overextended and disunified production. The self-revelation of Mr. Bill's character through his dialectal, homey-philosophy reportings to Philemon Perch has drawn just praise, but in a more controlled overall structure, it could justly gain more.

With the significant later excisions and such a clear split of narrative interest and modes, no single story illustrates so well and so graphically the Old-Southwest-humor-to-local-color development that Johnston is said so superbly to reflect. Of course, local color was never absent from his tales, and even *Georgia Sketches* in 1864 was advertised as containing stories of humor *and* pathos. A movement generally from rather rollicking realism to more idealized conception, from humorous forthrightness to quaint and genteel charm is definitely observable, however, and "Investigations Concerning Mr. Jonas Lively" is something of a fossilized microcosm of this larger process. Vivid, original, self-sufficient characterization did give way in Johnston's work to "characters whose minor eccentricities furnish a convenient peg on which to hang local color material"[8] in conventional plots. He was to make extensive use of courtship, marriage, and recovered wills in his future fiction, but "originals" like the early Jonas Lively became less and less subject to Johnston's investigation.

Mark Twain claimed that it was the influence of Sir Walter Scott that "made every gentleman in the South a major or a colonel, or a general or a judge, before the war," but who or whatever is to blame, Johnston could scarcely have escaped having one of these titled gentlemen as one of his title characters. As a reasonably realistic portrayer of early nineteenth-century rural Georgia and a fine perceiver of humorous potential, he certainly could not overlook the district militia organization whose ludicrous activities had in fact given rise to countless military titles and to pompousness in many of their possessors. Moses Grice of Dukesborough was "kurnel" of the Fourteenth Regiment, Georgia Militia, but the glory that he sought to attract to himself in "The Expensive Treat of Colonel Moses Grice" is not martial. With much show and self-importance, Colonel Grice brings the Great World-renowned Circus to an ecstatic Dukesborough, but he overreaches himself by tricking Mr. Bill Williams and is put in his place before the whole town when the duping tables are immediately turned on him.

The militia had already been too much put into the American literary field for much originality to be granted to Colonel Grice, and the well-known circus hoax of sending out a performer disguised as a drunk had been appropriated by the Old Southwest humorists at least as early as William Tappan Thompson's "The Great Attraction" (1845).[9] Johnston's combination of the two is rather unusual and effective, however, and while he cannot be put in the same category as Meadows, Lorriby, and Lively, Moses Grice deserves a recorded place among Dukesborough's more memorable inhabitants. Like Josiah Lorriby, his own words and actions are allowed more than usual to define the character, and since his actions here relate almost entirely to the circus, the reader is treated to an amusing characterization of a whole excited community as well.

Colonel Moses Grice was a man of thirty-five years, a substantial planter who, although he had been to the theater three times in Augusta, had not yet fulfilled his great desire of seeing a circus. He

had a wife, but no child (a point on which he was, perhaps, a little sore), was not in debt, was hospitable, an encourager (especially in words) of public and private enterprises, and enthusiastically devoted, though without experience in wars, to the military profession, which—if he might use the expression—he would call his second wife. Off the muster-field he habitually practiced that affability which is pleasant because so rare to see in the warrior class. When in full uniform and at the head of the regiment, with girt sword and pistol-holster, he did indeed look like a man not to be fooled with; and the sound of his voice in utterance of military orders was such as to show that he intended those orders to be heard and obeyed. When the regiment was disbanded, the sternness would depart from his mien, and, though yet unstripped of weapons and regalia, he would smile blandly, as if to reassure spectators that, for the present, the danger was over, and persons might approach without apprehension. (pp. 247 - 248)

Although he traveled ahead to meet the circus and build up his knowledge about its people and performances, the Colonel is no more sure of its animals than the excited, admonishing Dukesborough mother who yells, "Stay behind there, you, Jack, and you, Susan! You want to git eat up by them camels and varmints?" He receives a temporary setback from the hyena during his boastful conducting of a tour of the animal cages:

Just as the party was about to pass on, the wretched beast, stopping for a moment, his snout pressed to the roof, uttered several short, loud, hoarse, terrific howls. Miss Spouter screamed, Miss Pea laughed hysterically, and Colonel Grice, before he knew it, was on the outside of his knot of followers. Recovering himself—for he was without his sword and pistol-holster—he stepped quickly back to the front, looked threateningly, and afterward disdainfully, at the hyena, who had resumed his walks, and said:

"You rhinocerous varmint, you! Thinkin' of them graveyards you've robbed and hungry for some more of 'em,' ah! These is live folks, my boy; and they ain't quite ready for you yit, nor won't be for some time, I hope." Then he led on to the monkeys. (pp. 253 - 254)

Grice's real setback comes after he has treated himself to getting Bill Williams, now married and the father of twins, to try to stop the hoax drunk from entering the ring. Believing himself to be given the signal but deserved honor of being invited down for a public drink of whiskey with one of the clowns, Grice can only cut loose with string after string of abusive epithets when he realizes he has been duped: "You spotted-back, striped-legged, streaked-faced, speckled-b-breasted, p'inted-hatted, streaked-fac-ed, speckled b-breast—. . . ." Unfortunately, though, and especially so in this case, Johnston again extends his tale too far beyond this natural climax.

The language of the good Colonel does not compare either in kind or in effect with the various languages of Billy Moon in Johnston's story by this name. One of its author's favorites, this short piece again recounts a single incident in which a vain, self-elevated man is put humorously in his place. Reflecting the combative pride of the Middle Georgian of his boyhood and making use of the formal fights which were the highlights of militia muster days, Johnston in "The Various Languages of Billy Moon" is once more close to the older humorists, most notably to A. B. Longstreet. One has therefore met the type before, but Oglethorpe Josh Green, who has to come to Dukesborough to fight because he's whipped everyone in his own district, can be met only in Johnston's tale. Whom the boastful "O.J.G.," as he is called, meets in combat is Billy Moon, deaf and dumb and possessed of enormous strength. O.J.G. cannot ultimately cope with the latter attribute, but he is particularly taken aback by the former, which results in a strange and wonderful, and for O.J.G. a totally unfathomable, system of communication.

Finally talked into a friendly wrestle with Moon, Oglethorpe Josh Green is readily defeated, and still somewhat in multiple shock he inquires of Billy's translator if it is possible to give the victor a handshake. The result Johnston describes, for him, most burlesquely. O.J.G. felt tears rush into his eyes, hit his knees hard together, "and when Billy had let his hand go, held it up, letting it hang loosely, regarded it for a moment as something entirely foreign to himself, gradually pulled its fingers apart with his other hand, and seemed

gratified and somewhat surprised that such a thing could be done."
When, after the parties have had a drink together, O.J.G. prepared to
take his leave, he carefully placed his hands in his pockets. Then, with
a long, final, earnest look at Billy, he requested quietly of the inter-
preter, "Tell it farewell for me!" Remaining from that time much
closer to home, grown quieter and much more meditative, O.J.G.
would nevertheless occasionally recall the events of that day:

> "Gentlemen, it were a kind of a egiot, and it were grippy as a wise, and it
> were supple as a black-snake, and it were strong as a mule and a bull both
> putten together. And, gentlemen," he would add, "egiot as it were, it were
> smarter'n any man ever I see; and as for its langwidges—well, gentlemen,
> they wa'n't no eend to its warious langwidges." (p. 86)

Johnston performs the storyteller's tasks well in "The Various
Languages of Billy Moon," which is one of the few of his tales capable
of eliciting a real stomach laugh. He also excels in "The Early Majority of Mr. Thomas Watts," but here the elicitation is smiling sympathy
or amused identification. In this little sketch, which was Johnston's
favorite platform piece, he returns again to the subject of school life in
Dukesborough. While pedagogues—and especially a female
teacher—have important roles in the story, the focus is upon thirteen-
year-old Thomas Watts. Thirteen-year-old Richard Malcolm
Johnston, much regretting the difference of ages, had "had a sort of
worship" for Miss Rebecca Platt, a school assistant in Powelton, and
this he recalled in telling the bittersweet tale of young "Mr. Thomas
Watts" who "fondly, entirely, madly loved Miss Julia Louisa Wilkins,
the mistress and head of the Dukesborough Female Institution."

Thomas Watts was numbered among the eight children mothered
by that excellent woman so concerned about the camels when Colonel
Grice's famous circus had come to town. Because the now-fatherless
Watts children were of both sexes but wore hand-me-downs in-
discriminately, it was not always possible to discern readily the sex of
any one of them, and there was for a time some fear that Thomas
might develop a repugnance to females from "his remembrance of
the long confusion of the public mind touching his own sex." With the
bursting forth of "all the fresh young worship of that young but manly
heart" for Miss Wilkins, all such fear was dispelled, however. From
the fortuitous beginning of helping to get the fire started at the girls'
school one day, Thomas came to render regular service at Miss
Wilkins's "institution," rather to the detriment of his own schoolwork
at Mr. Cordy's establishment. His sister Susan, realizing her brother's
growing passion, characterized his actions and ambitions as "perfect-

ly redickerlous," but Thomas had no doubt that his great love was requited. Abandoning his plan of choosing a male guardian, he determined to consummate the union with Miss Wilkins on his fourteenth birthday and take his bride back to Vermont—all of this to be accomplished on his bride-to-be's cash. Susan, however, told her mother of the state of affairs, and when Mrs. Watts discovered in Thomas's secret box his love poetry and a formal written proposal as well as a small piece of Miss Wilkins's sweet soap, it was almost more than motherhood could bear: " 'It's enough to make anybody sick at the stomach. I know'd the child didn't have much sense; but I didn't know he was a clean-gone fool.' " Thomas was consequently called upon to bear a most unceremonious whipping, and he but narrowly escaped having "pantaloonses" put back on him. He would delay manhood for a while, he reckoned.

Johnston hit perhaps his most universal chord in this autobiographical tale. Mr. Thomas Watts's earnest wish to forget his early majority is, for several reasons, not likely to be shared by Johnston's readers. Miss Julia Louisa Wilkins left Dukesborough not long after the events related, and rumor reported her death about two years later. Little Mr. Thomas Watts deserves to live memorably on, however.

III *Census Taking Continued: The Less Vital Figures*

The contents of that hypothetical collection of the most-worthy-to-be-preserved of Johnston's stories, a volume that Johnston scholars seem compelled to construct, are about as various as the editions of *Dukesborough Tales*. And such variation within reasonable limits is, as Josiah Lorriby might say, "jest as such as it are likely and as sich should be." While all of them are not in everyone's volume, most of the six sketches discussed above are in most. The remaining ten constituents of *Dukesborough Tales* are, on the other hand, much less frequently included. In them the flaws noted above are more evident, the shortcomings less redeemed. They too contribute to the annals and to the census of Dukesborough, but what they have to report is more properly housed in a bureau of less vital figures.

The other stories that come closest to making significant contributions to the Dukesborough census are "Mr. Williamson Slippey and His Salt," "The Pursuit of Mr. Adiel Slack," "Judge Mike's Court," and "Mr. Neelus Peeler's Conditions." In all four, though not equally successfully in all and in none so notably as in "The Various Languages" or "The Early Majority," Johnston achieves that

felicitous blend of "situational and verbal humor"[10] that
characterizes his best productions. Significantly, all except the last,
"Mr. Neelus Peeler's Conditions," which was his first paid story,
emerged from the earliest period of his literary efforts.

"Mr. Williamson Slippey and His Salt" is one of the few Johnston
tales not set in or around Dukesborough, and one of the few that is set
as late as the 1860s. Though an avaricious one, Mr. Slippey is,
however, a native of Dukesborough, a son of that community who has
"made good" as an Atlanta merchant by means not so good—namely
and mainly by the hoarding of salt, a commodity that became
precious in the South during the Civil War. Mr. Slippey, who appropriately ages himself to escape conscription, refuses to release any
of his stockpile on reasonable terms even to friends to whom he owes
his present position. Lying one night in a drunken stupor, Slippey is
confronted by one of these friends with vivid visions of hell, and these,
combined with the immediate circumstance of an accidental fire, are
sufficient to make the selfish ingrate end his business operations. The
general description of Williamson Slippey and especially the account of his toddy time give him ample amusing individuality, but his
humorous characterization is hardly enhanced by Johnston's use of
didactic dream-motif machinery. Johnston's concern in this tale is
more with characterization than with plot, but he also attempts here,
to the detriment of characterization and humor, to depict an effect of
the Civil War on the Southern people which he personally found most
disturbing.

Familar motifs, this time the trickster Yankee and a courtship
rivalry, appear also in "The Pursuit of Mr. Adiel Slack." In this tale a
long-standing female friendship is threatened by a man's false affections until, entertainingly though expectedly, the trickster is himself
tricked and the friendship reestablished. Although they may be
regarded as anxious unmarried types, Misses Georgiana Pea and
Angeline Spouter achieve considerably more distinctiveness than the
swindler and bigamist who vies for their respective riches. Thirty-
year-old Angeline Spouter, daughter of the owner of Spouter's Hotel
(where, by the way, Mr. Bill Williams boarded while he was a
bachelor), finds that beautiful curls and preferential treatment at the
hotel are insufficient to match the attractions of a large bust and the
promise of a thousand acres of good land which matrimony with
thirty-year-old Georgiana Pea holds forth. Although the marriage
takes place, Georgiana does not allow the union to be consummated

and removes from his luggage the money and valuables Slack steals when he does not find the land forthcoming. Miss Pea and Miss Spouter appear in other Dukesbourough tales, but their essential identity is realized in connection with this one great love of their lives. Potential publishers, Johnston said, saw in the tale "more innuendoes and things 'hinted at,' than, so far as I know, Miss Pea & Miss Spouter imagined."[11] Such vital suggestiveness he would, unfortunately because successfully, strive more and more to avoid.

Characterizations based upon occupational types achieve enough individuality to call "Judge Mike's Court" and "Mr. Neelus Peeler's Conditions," two quite different stories, to appropriate similar notice. In the former story, Johnston has a social message, just as he may have had in his pedagogical tales and as he did in the sketch about Williamson Slippey. This time his concern is a corrupt judicial system, and he makes the concern and his points blatant by opposing two sets of characters and employing a moral mouthpiece. Mr. Parkinson and Mr. Overton are aligned as observational characters on the side of right and intelligence, and Mr. Mobley, the defense attorney in the trial depicted, is the active hero in that cause. Their more-than-nominal adversaries are the incompetent judge, Littleberry W. Mike; the sheriff, John Sanks; and the prosecutor, Elam Sandidge, who is the real mover of the corrupt bunch. Right, of course, prevails, and although the facts are rendered with realism and humor, the overwhelming purpose of social criticism is all too obvious. Again it is, however, the "bad" characters (but Johnston's are seldom entirely bad) who prevail in the reader's memory—the most notable being the inept and touchy Judge Mike, best revealed perhaps in the burlesquely reported sneezing incident in his court which involves Allen Thigpen of Goosepond school fame.

Mr. Neelus Peeler, who had married one of the Goosepond school's female students, is a "called" preacher who is as inept in this calling as he was in that of a plantation overseer. The plain fact is that Neelus is lazy, and his frequently lamented "conditions," the many shortcomings of members of his family which are such a hindrance to him, are but his evasions of the truth. The most interesting incident in "Mr. Neelus Peeler's Conditions" does not focus on Neelus himself, but involves rather his lazy son Elijah's getting drunk at the militia muster at which he was to keep his uncle Sam sober. This tale is the one for which Johnston received Sidney Lanier's experienced tutelage, and a publication-pointed, local-color consciousness is evident right down to the nice neat resolution of the quaint, idiosyncratic problem. The plot line is stronger than it had been in Johnston's tales to this time, and the story's character development is praiseworthy. Here, however, Johnston makes less of humorous than he does of pathetic potential; here, and it is a significant shift, he seems to seek more a smiling sympathy than simply a smile.[12] Under other conditions than these, Neelus Peeler would have been a more vital Dukesborough figure.

Yet another Dukesborough story that makes use of militia muster day is "King William and His Armies," which includes several familiar Dukesborough characters. The principal incident of the tale is the challenge and honor-satisfying defeat of Colonel Moses Grice by Mr. Bill Williams in a fight following the muster drill, but this tale is far removed from any of Longstreet's or really any of the other of Johnston's stories dealing with such combat. Chronicling quite consciously and deliberately the marital and domestic history of Bill Williams and the "meloncholy" of Miles Bunkly, Johnston is quite evidently the proprietary local-color writer, the careful seeker after effects based on the quaint peculiarities of his chosen place and its people. His conception and his rendering are idealized and genteel, and a play for sentiment is the obvious *modus operandi*.

The five remaining stories that appeared specifically as Dukesborough tales are all characterized by the sentiment, the attitudes, and the resultant literary features that have come to be associated with local-color and popular magazine pieces of the later nineteenth century. In one, "The Organ-Grinder," Johnston slips flatly into sentimentality in relating the sad history of an Italian violinist and his daughter who enter briefly but affectingly into the life of Dukesborough. No humor and practically no local color come to the rescue of this piece, as they do to varying degrees in the four other tales, all concerned in some way with what was to become Johnston's favorite and ultimately overused subject: courtship and marriage.

"The Jonce Trammel Compromise" is the unexceptional account of how a compromise is finally effected between Mr. Trammel, who drinks too much, and Mrs. Trammel, who weaves too much, respective habits which the other partner finds obnoxious. "The Beazley Twins" shows the effecting of two marriages, with supposedly unexpected pairings, of an uncle and his nephew with a widow and an orphan. Having more to recommend it is "Puss Tanner's Defence" because of the fine local-color descriptions of the countryside, accounts of unique church activities, and the characterization of Aunt Polly Peacock. The plot, which concerns the clearing of Puss Tanner's female honor, is based upon what seems to the modern reader a very trivial incident. Interesting and realistic as are the reactions of various social levels and individuals of the community and, specifically, the refusal to admit the testimony of a Negro, all is predictably resolved in appropriate marriages at the end.

"Old Friends and New," although it was first published in 1872, is a fitting story on which to end a consideration of Dukesborough tales. The longest of the "Dukesboroughs," as Johnston called them, and the final story of the final Baltimore edition, it exhibits a special effort to refer to and draw together and connect a large number of the actions and characters of other Dukesborough tales. If "Investigations Concerning Mr. Jonas Lively" stands as a good single example of Johnston's process of transition from more realistic humor to appealing local-color sentiment, "Old Friends and New" may stand as the example of the achievement of the change.

Seemingly now taking the advice given him by the forward-looking editor of *Harper's Magazine* in 1860, Johnston in this story steers away from the "grotesque and ridiculous" and pictures instead in the persons of George Overton and the Parkinson family "the intellectual and refined side of Southern character," "Southern men and women of the highest and purest type."[13] By having the Virginia lawyer Overton teach a school while he is at Chestnut Grove, the Parkinson plantation home, Johnston can effectively introduce characters of lower social classes as well. With this basic situation he can also, and does with some effective contrasts, deal extensively with two of his favorite subjects, education and romantic matchmaking. Descriptions of two events emerging from these interests, the proceedings of the midsummer school commencement and a country wedding, possess value as social history. Descriptions of Overton's practice of the "Rockby" system of education and of the Lucy Parkinson-George Overton love affair, sadly aided by the death of little Jack Parkinson, come very close, however, to sentimentality. And rather than providing the humorous relief that might have been a salvation, the Bill Williams and Betsy Ann Acry-"Karline" Thigpen courtship becomes yet another competing narrative thread. In "Old Friends and New," Johnston still has his old structural problems, and he offers no strong new characters in sufficient compensation.

In "Old Friends and New" Johnston gives extensive authorial expression to the nostalgia that came more and more to be the fountainhead of his literary output:

> Blessed old times! They had their errors and their evils. Many of these have been corrected, and others, I trust, will be in reasonable time. Would that what were some of their greatest goods, the simplicity of ancient manners and the cordiality of social intercourse, could have been found to be not uncongenial with our advancing civilization!(pp. 180 - 181)

It was, of course, the latter that he most sought to preserve amidst increasing uncongeniality, and this preservation is valuable in and of itself. But it was the errors and the evils, which for a time he was able to view with humor and detachment, that contribute most to the literary value of *Dukesborough Tales*.

IV   Dukesborough: *A Final Figuring*

The assessments of Johnston's best-known work that were cited at the beginning of this chapter are corroborated by a close scrutiny of the full complement of *Dukesborough Tales*. Late twentieth-century readers are not likely to admire the "sweetness," "wholesomeness," and "innocence" of the tales as did their predecessors, nor are they likely to echo nineteenth-century praise of the tales' "satisfying realism" and universality. A certain "whimsical grace" and quaint charm may still be apprehended, however, and attempt should be made to appreciate a knowledgeable contemporary's opinion that *Dukesborough Tales* added "a new field of character-painting to the range of American fiction."[14] Both the nineteenth-century assessment of the "Dukesboroughs" as "well-told stories"[15] and the twentieth-century view of them as "inexpert anecdotes"[16] seem extreme misses of the mark. Surely the characters to which some of these tales and sketches give life and the "peculiar and telling way" in which this life is given make Johnston's most famous volume "something more."[17]

At the time of Johnston's death the Baltimore *Sun* saw the Dukesborough tales as "classics of lowly Georgia life which will hold their place permanently in American literature as faithful though humorous delineations of the period and types to which they relate."[18] Such a conclusion is predicated upon the idea that, as Stark Young put it, although "the primary function of a society is not to produce art, . . . a primary function of its art is to express that society."[19] For this reason if for no other—by virtue both of its substance and its style—*Dukesborough Tales* has valid claim to the status of a minor classic.

CHAPTER 3

Later Tales and Sketches

A LTHOUGH only the first sixteen of his stories were ex-pressly labeled Dukesborough tales, Richard Malcolm Johnston as a writer of fiction never really produced anything else. For eighty-two of his eighty-three published pieces of short fiction, there could be no more appropriate collection title than a combination of two of his own choices—*Dukesborough Tales: Old Times in Middle Georgia*.

Dukesborough is the hub, the central point of reference, of the Middle Georgia which is Johnston's fictional world. Widely acknowl-edged by nineteenth-century Georgians as a distinctive region within their state, the territory of Middle Georgia has been variously delineated. Frequently the term has been used in general reference to that portion of Georgia within the triangle formed by the cities of Macon, Athens, and Augusta,[1] the last of which was the undisputed Meccan metropolis of the region. Joel Chandler Harris designated Middle Georgia as the territory between the Ogeechee and Ocmulgee Rivers, some three thousand square miles divided by the Oconee River, while Charles Forster Smith's boundaries made the region one hundred miles east to west and sixty miles north to south.[2] The territory to which Johnston's local-color stories give existence is more limited than any of these, but the geological and agricultural features of his fictional world accurately reflect those of the seventeen-county area which has also been said, topographically and politically, to form Middle Georgia.[3]

While climate and topography are, of course, influential and im-portant factors, Johnston's overriding interest was in the people of Middle Georgia, a society that he along with other contemporary observers viewed as unique. Why "so many of the published character-sketches of the South" originated in this section he was at no loss to explain:

Middle Georgia. . . , settled by immigrants from the older states, chiefly Virginia and North Carolina, was found to be as salubrious as fertile. Its undulations of wide uplands and narrow lowlands watered by swiftly running small rivers and creeks, its thick forests beneath which was a soil radiant with redness and teeming with fecundity, made it as pleasant an abode for man as any in the whole South. Therein families of various degrees of culture and property got homesteads, not many less than two hundred, and fewer more than one thousand, acres. Almost every one owned one or two, almost none more than fifty, slaves. Fewer distinctions were among their dwelling-houses. The salubrity of the climate made settlements almost everywhere equally secure. Therefore those of all conditions became close neighbors of one another, and intimacies necessarily arose destined to produce important results variant, not only from those in other Southern States, but from those in the low-lying wire-grass and seaboard region of Georgia. . . .

In a community constituted like that of Middle Georgia whatever was striking in individuality found unobstructed development in social intercourse that was untrammeled except by unwritten laws that excluded only what was indecent and unmanly. There were manifestations of the exuberant freedom of the rustic in that happy region that made him interesting enough to become the hero of a brief story of life and manners. He differed from the rustic of the seaboard as much as any French Switzer differs from the Italian or the German beyond the impassable mountain between them. . . .[4]

The folks of Middle Georgia—their eccentricities and their activities—are the quintessence of Johnston's fiction. While his tales may be categorized on various formal or technical grounds, classification on the bases of character type and social activity is more usual because it is more essential. This chapter surveys Johnston's remaining short fiction chronologically by collection, but within this scheme necessarily appear revealing character and institutional groupings.

The limited setting to which he or his talents restricted him accounts for Johnston's strengths as well as his major weaknesses as a writer. The clearly defined because constantly recurred to locale gives reality and effectiveness to his characters and situations; because of the exclusiveness of the setting, however, the people and their lives become familiar to the point of triviality.[5] Because Johnston went neither beyond nor beneath the pleasant, amusing surface life of Middle Georgia, his re-created rural world is the source both of appealing reality and appalling banality.[6] And from beginning to end, Dukesborough was the hub of this universe.

I   Mr. Absalom Billingslea and Other Georgia Folk

Published by Harper & Brothers in 1888, *Mr. Absalom Billingslea
and Other Georgia Folk* contains a statement of Johnston's literary
aims and fourteen of his sketches, at least twelve of which had
appeared previously in "the magazines," as Johnston put it.[7] The title
of the collection evinces its folksy character, and in the preface the
author acknowledges the autobiographical basis and fond, nostalgic
bias of his productions. He has attempted, he says, "to illustrate some
phases of old-time rural life in middle Georgia,. . . to show how
superior was the character to what might have been expected from the
dialect of the people."

These people, he goes on to say, he loves "not less" for some of their
"oddities of deportment and dialect." Fundamentally a humorist, he
loves them all the more for this, of course. As was true for the local
colorists in general, eccentricity of character is the stock-in-trade of
the author of *Mr. Absalom Billingslea*. Mr. Ephrodtus Twilley is
possessed of "suicidal tendencies," Riley Hood experiences "historic
doubts," and Mr. Pink Fluker has a "hotel experience." A proper
name, usually attached in some way to an intriguing attributive noun,
dominates the title of every piece.

In this first collection after *Dukesborough Tales* Johnston's favorite
subjects and situations are established with corroborative as well as
prophetic clearness. Foremost among these are courtship and
marriage, to which Johnston was led by personal predilection as much
as by the demands of popular literary taste. Tales of triumphant
courtship, the "happy-pairing" resolution of various difficulties and
misunderstandings, dominate *Mr. Absalom Billingslea and Other
Georgia Folk*. Not content with a single, direct affair, Johnston makes
frequent use of multiple, disguised courtships in order to present an
intendedly surprising lineup of blissful couples at the end. Widows,
old bachelors, and orphans are his favorite and the favored par-
ticipants in such goings-on. Such are the basic outline and the casts for
"The Brief Embarrassment of Mr. Iverson Blount," "The Rivalries of
Mr. Toby Gillam," "The Wimpy Adoptions," "A Critical Accident to
Mr. Absalom Billingslea," and "The Mediations of Mr. Archie Kit-
trell." This last tale exhibits, in addition, two recurrent social interests
of Johnston's: religious or church activity (especially the Baptist-
Methodist denominational rivalry) and judicial or court activity in
Middle Georgia.

In three more stories—"Martha Reid's Lovers," "Mr. Thomas

Chivers's Boarder," and "The Stubblefield Contingents"—there is a taste of love and marriage, but not so light a taste. In them, property-hungry villains are pictured in darker hues than is usual for the Johnston spectrum. And Negro characters, albeit in varying roles, are important in two of the three. Two other stories, "The Hotel Experience of Mr. Pink Fluker" and "Rev. Rainford Gunn and the Arab Chief," also include or involve romantic attraction, but each of these productions is most memorable for its conflict between males, the first for the duping of a naive farmer-moved-to-town and the second for the triumph of an unsophisticated country preacher over his city antagonist.

Only four of the tales in *Mr. Absalom Billingslea* escape the "loving" point of Johnston's pen. Two are "Dr. Hinson's Degree," which draws upon the old Middle Georgia antagonism between settlers from North Carolina and those from Virginia, and "Historic Doubts of Riley Hood," which, reporting an incident of childhood, recalls young Thomas Watts of *Dukesborough* fame. More memorable are "The Suicidal Tendencies of Mr. Ephrodtus Twilley," the humorous story of a marital relationship in which the wife emerges firmly triumphant, and "Moll and Virgil," a lachrymose testimonial to the loyalty of Negro slaves.

For a representative introduction to Johnston's short fiction, or to local-color short fiction, or to late nineteenth-century popular American magazine fiction, no special reading recommendations for *Mr. Absalom Billingslea* need to be made. The tales in this collection that show meaningful deviation from these norms do so mostly, as in the case of *Dukesborough Tales*, to the extent that they have retained some of the robust realism of the productions of Old Southwest humorists. Thus, although there is sportive bemusement in all and although love or right or truth triumphs affectingly in all, a few of the stories do provide scenes whose genuineness and spontaneous, vigorous humor are impressive. Take, for example, the vanquishing of the village rowdy by the Reverend Rainford Gunn:

The preacher took a step rearward, doubled his fist and dealt upon the assailant's breast a blow that prostrated him upon his back at the foot of the pulpit. Snatching his cane as he was falling, he raised it aloft.

"Now try to rise if you dare," cried Mr. Gunn, whose eyes were floods of tears, "an' I'll scatter that pulpit with your brains."

"My God!" cried Rogers.

"Them's the words, sir; them's the wery words."

. . ."Know the Lord's pra'ar?"

"Of course I do, Mr. Gunn."
"Say it."
Rogers hesitated.
"Say it, I tell you."
"Won't you give a man time to think it up?"
"I thought you knowed it. Said you did."
"I do, Mr. Gunn, but it's been so long since—"
"Blaze away, and go as fur as you ken."

" 'Now I lay me down to sleep,
I pray—' "[8]

And if, in "The Hotel Experience of Mr. Pink Fluker," Mr. Fluker "did not become fully convinced that his mathematical education was not advanced quite enough for all the exigencies of hotel-keeping," the reader has no doubt on that score. Pink, who has figured Matt Pike's bill as $33, listens in uncomprehending bewilderment to Matt's flimflam amending of the charges to $1:

"Jes' so. Now look here," drawing from his pocket a paper. "Itom one. Twenty-eight dinners at half a dollar makes fourteen dollars, don't it? Jes' so. Twenty-five breakfasts at a quarter makes six an' a quarter, which make dinners an' breakfasts twenty an' a quarter. Foller me up as I go up, Pink. Twenty-five suppers at a quarter makes six an' a quarter, an' which them added to the twenty an' a quarter, makes them twenty-six an' a half. Foller, Pink, an' if you ketch me in any mistakes in the k'yar'n' an' addin' p'int it out. Twenty-two an' a half beds—an' I say *half*, Pink, because you 'member one night when them A'gusty lawyers got here 'bout midnight on their way to co't, ruther'n have you too bad cramped, I ris to make way for two of 'em; yit as I had one good nap, I didn't think I ought to put that down but for half. Them makes five dollars half an' seb'n pence, an' which k'yar'd on to the tother twenty-six an' a half, fetches the whole cabool to jes' thirty-two dollars an' seb'n pence. But I made up my mind I'd fling out that seb'n pence, an' jes call it a dollar even money, an' which here's the solid silver.[9]

II   The Primes and Their Neighbors

Carrying the subtitle *Ten Tales of Middle Georgia, The Primes and Their Neighbors* (D. Appleton and Company, 1891) exhibits more ore from Johnston's Georgia mine. All of its stories but one, "The Durance of Mr. Dickerson Prime," had appeared previously in such periodicals as *Harper's Magazine, Harper's Bazaar, Harper's Weekly, The Cosmopolitan,* and *The Century.* The collection title, the epigraph, the preface, and the individual story titles again immediately make the autobiographical, nostalgic, humanistic bases manifest. Again, lamenting their diminution and modification since "the Confederate War," Johnston points in the preface to the "striking rustic individualities" of the simple folk of Middle Georgia. And again he draws sketches which, though mostly imaginary, "are in harmony with the rural society which the author remembers as a lad, and later as a young lawyer."

Modern reader-reviewers of the book would find no quarrel with some of the assessments of *The Primes* by contemporary reviewers. The *New York Times* claimed, for example, that "not one of the tales is stupid" and that "nearly every one contains a character either original or so pleasantly drawn that it assumes distinctiveness as an individuality."[10] The *New York Commercial Advertiser* similarly praised the winning oddity of these quaint people who acted as well as talked in a sort of dialect,[11] and most objectively perhaps, *The Critic* pointed out the significance of the collection for the social historian.[12] The assessment in *The Dial* is hardly so palatable, however. Time has not pushed Johnston to a place ahead of Bret Harte, and the twentieth century is not likely to agree that the stories in this collection are "examples of the best sort of realism,—that which is faithful to the facts of life, but which also recognizes the duty of ordering the facts in forms of artistic symmetry."[13]

One symmetrical form that does appear—or reappear—is the formulaic one of courtship conflict and resolution. At least one of the "common Johnstonian elements" of "widowers who want to remarry, children who fear such remarriages, mistaken ideas of who is courting whom, and friends whose strained friendship is healed"—situational or structural devices which Clara Ruth Coleman Wood sees in "The Experiment of Miss Sally Cash"[14]—also appears in "Mr. Gibble Colt's Ducks," "Mr. Joseph Pate and His People," and "The Self-Protection of Mr. Littleberry Roach." Less disguised courtships and younger love matches are part of "The Durance of Mr. Dickerson Prime" and "New Discipline at Rock Spring." Rounding out *The Primes* in less predictable and more praiseworthy fashion are "The Combustion of Jim Rakestraw" and "The Humors of Jacky Bundle," tales involving physical violence in the tradition of Old Southwest humor; "Travis and Major Jonathan Wilby," another account of the touching loyalty of a former Negro slave for his master; and "The Pursuit of the Martyns," a longer, darker piece which, like some other of Johnston's longer fiction, is a story of murder and deception.

Although he was essentially and even stereotypically the romantic Southerner, Johnston was not, however, all "moonlight and magnolias" in his matchmaking. In spite of, by now, the singular unexcitement of his romantic plots, almost all of the courtship tales in *The Primes* have a redeeming humor, which in some instances comes from an admirably organic merging of situation and character. Many of the tales also exhibit a realistic recognition of the material considerations, especially increased land holdings, that underlie campaigns for matrimony. Not capable of many diverse manifestations, this element rings less genuine than does the humor, however.

Tall, slender, humorous Singleton Hooks in "The Experiment of Miss Sally Cash" is a good, extended example of Johnston's skill and delight in describing the amazing transformations of a widow or widower who sets out to win another mate, and Mr. Pate, who appears in this story as well as the one bearing his name, is a garrulous old man whom Johnston was to develop into one of his most felicitous characters. Mr. Dickerson Prime in the story about his "durance" is also well drawn. For his thwarting of true love for reasons of social ambition, Mr. Prime is exposed to smallpox and banished at gunpoint by his wife to the plantation cotton-house. Samuel Cox also uses a gun to impressive purposes in "New Discipline at Rock Spring," but here Johnston is too busy propounding his "gentlemanly" educational methods to let much humor through the schoolhouse door.

Although the event leads directly to matrimony in "The Self-Protection of Mr. Littleberry Roach," there is boisterous humor in Mr. Roach's being stuck with a stout brass pin as he sits benignly in church absorbing expressions of gratitude for his generous contributions to the building program. Such a prank and the deflating humor of physical discomfiture are part of the frontier humor of the Old Southwest, which appears in rather full-blown form in two other tales. "The Humors of Jacky Bundle" with its detailed description of militia muster day and the climactic altercation between Jacky and Reddick Sanders is reminiscent of some of Longstreet's as well as some of Johnston's own earlier sketches. Red Sanders, who has his nose used to dig up the ground, comes off rather better, however, than Jim Rakestraw, whose fate is revealed in "The Combustion of Jim Rakestraw." For this tale Johnston, who seldom failed to include an epigraph for his fictional pieces, uses the line from Pope's *Windsor Forest*, "But brief his joy; he feels the fiery wound." If not stylistically congruous with the tale, the epigraph provides an apt description of the antagonist in the climactic episode: Rakestraw, a large and lazy scoundrel (his "foot was so big that some said it had no business to be called a foot at all, and so they called it a thirteen incher"), is discovered pilfering Len Cane's fish-traps and is set afire by a well-aimed load of fat meat from Len's well-primed gun.

The story of Len and Jim is a framed tale told by Mr. Pate, that "aged historian" of Dukesborough and the "old" friend of a faithful younger auditor and narrator who much resembles "our" old friend Philemon Perch. "Travis and Major Jonathan Wilby," told in a direct and fetching first-person, also exhibits virtuosity of narration, but its tone, subject-matter, and purpose are quite different. One of the few of Johnston's tales set after the Civil War, it is the account of a pleasant chance stay at Major Wilby's plantation and the gradual learning of the sad facts of Wilby's life and present condition: although he believes himself restored to a life almost like that of antebellum times, the gentlemanly Wilby, his mind deranged from war injuries and the loss of his lady love, lives under the tender care and on the legal property of Travis, once the Major's slave and now his devoted if dissembling guardian. "I had been witness," reports the narrator, "of the old affectionateness of slaves continuing unhurt by the war and emancipation; but now . . . I felt that I had been in the presence of a majesty, in its kind, higher than I had believed possible to humanity in any condition."[15] Both because of subject and successful execution, Johnston's tale compares quite favorably with his friend Thomas Nelson Page's "Marse Chan." Travis may be an overly romanticized part of the myth of the Old South, but at least one of the old slave's comments to the narrator is short of sentimental ideality: "But den you know, marster, f'om your own expeunce, ef you married, a man needn't be tellin' his wife ev'ythin' he know."[16]

The reader's knowledge of the facts is effectively delayed in "The Pursuit of the Martyns" just as it is in "Travis and Major Jonathan Wilby," and the tone of this long story is also serious, even somber. In the tale are recurrent Johnstonian elements such as the attraction of the sexes, land and property greed, garrulous old men, and court proceedings. Less usual, however, are the two murders and especially, very atypical for Johnston, the meditative turning in of a character upon himself—in effect, a psychological study of guilt.[17] Pleasing in its deviations if not in its artistry, "The Pursuit of the Martyns" does not picture, as the epigraph to *The Primes* generally advertises, the "happy fields, unknown to noise and strife."

III   Mr. Fortner's Marital Claims and Other Stories

The "other" of *Mr. Fortner's Marital Claims and Other Stories* (D. Appleton and Company) are only four in number, this volume being one of two Johnston collections published in the fall of 1892. The only previously unpublished tale in the lot, the title story of this book, is in several ways also the most interesting and important.

The tales of this volume for the most part augment rather than advance Johnston's burgeoning picture of Middle Georgia life of the 1820s, '30s, and '40s. While some characters uniquely and even memorably transcend their patterns, much of the substance, the narrative form, and the created mood of this collection strike the regular Johnston reader as repetitious. If it is not Philemon Perch himself, for example, it is his double who recounts "A Moccasin Among the Hobbys" and "Old Gus Lawson." The latter, with its appealing portrait of Augustus Lawson, the slow, amiable, overaged schoolboy with his inexhaustible pockets and inimitable mime of a rabbit eating turnip greens, is generally reminiscent of "How Mr. Bill Williams Took the Responsibility." "Old Gus," who "have fell in love," is not able until the end of the story to discern exactly who is the object of his passion, but when with help he does, he, of course, wins her—the pretty but tongue-tied Miranda Attaway. "Little Joe" Hobby also finally gets his lady love, now a widowed mother, in "A Moccasin Among the Hobbys." Saving Maggy's baby from a dreadful reptile, he is granted her grateful hand, though for his heroic effort he pays the price of a part of his own snake-bitten thumb. That he himself performs and describes the amputation helps, however, to relieve this story of excessive sentiment, a shortcoming that the pathetic "A Surprise to Mr. Thompson Byers," another tale of widow and child, does not escape.

Mr. Byers is the scheming, land-greedy villain, and Stephen Shepherd the lawyer-hero of this piece, the understanding and affectionate counsel for Widow Rowell and her retarded son Sandy. In court, although it is done extralegally and through Sandy's uncomprehending agency, Shepherd convincingly vanquishes the evil Byers. This "surprise," which "puts" Mr. Byers "off" to Mississippi, is a savage attack upon him by Sandy, an attack which ends with Sandy's sinking his teeth deep into Byers's shoulder. And right there in Byers's shoulder, we are told in the realistic if exaggerated fashion of Old Southwestern humor, "they clung, even when his body was lifted by the sheriff and one of his bailiffs, and they had to be pried apart by the hands of both." [18]

A much worse fate is feared by the title character of "An Adventure of Mr. Joel Boozle," a rather striking tale which with its grostesqueness, humorous exaggeration, and playing-of-a-prank motif owes much to the frontier humorists. Mr. Boozle's adventure, "a remarkable experience" which occurs on one of his infrequent visits to town, is his brush with Poly Cobble, the deformed "'littlest, 'flictedest creetur that ever were born.'"[19] Cobble, elsewhere described as "those fragmentary parts of humanity," has a regular-sized head but grossly undeveloped other parts, and so appears to be almost nothing but a head pushed around by a Negro in a little 3' by 2' cart. To get a drink out of the appreciative Boozle, Mr. Frank convinces the gullible "piney-woods man" that Poly is a dangerous murderer who has been convicted "time and time ag'in" but who, they find, cannot be executed: "'Well, now, sir, the only thing about Poly Cobble that have any solid weight worth talkin' about is his head; and when the sheriff puts the rope 'round his neck and h'ists him up, and there he hangs a-gigglin' until the sheriff out o' disgust cut him down, put him in his cart, call Bob, and order em to take themselves out a' his sight. Bye-bye.'"[20]

Although some liberated twentieth-century readers might also find grotesqueness and claim another "bad joke" therein, Johnston presents a local color far different from the Poly Cobble variety in "Mr. Fortner's Marital Claims," a domestic tale of the attempted subjugation of a wife by her husband. Once more, complete with multiple and misinterpreted courtships, the claims and interests of romantic love loom large; indeed it is the disagreement over the choice of mates for their daughters that brings Mr. Fortner and his wife Mimy to their impasse. But it is the relationship of these two, and the important, affecting role of denominational religion in the relationship, that is the significant focus of the story. Johnston was drawing here, with only slight exaggeration, from Middle Georgia people and institutions he knew intimately, and he draws both is personal and his institutional portraits well. Jeremiah ("Jaymiah") Fortner, "from his very youngest manhood, had been tall, slender, dark, and religious,"[21] his religion being emphatically and dogmatically Baptist. "'I'm thankful to the good Lord for two things,'" he would on occasion reveal, "'and the first one of 'em is him a-makin' me a man 'stead of a woman, and second, him a-lettin' me be a Babtis' 'stead of a Meth'dis'.'"[22] No male in Dukesborough took more to heart "the sentiment of St. Paul the apostle concerning marital authority" than Mr. Fortner, and there had never been serious marital strife in the Fortner household—although, as the narrator smilingly notes, it was largely "because often [Fortner] had thought that he was leading when in fact he was being led by both an understanding and a discretion superior to his own."[23] This last observation is made unmistakably clear when in the climactic church conference or congregational meeting Mr. Fortner attempts to indict his wife for insubordination but is, with her public rejoinder, himself crushed by the indictment. Jeremiah Fortner has learned a good lesson, and so has, Johnston would feel, the reader. But what the reader has learned about the early to mid-century marital and religious life of Middle Georgia is ultimately more satisfying than the abstract moral lesson which it has been used to embody.

IV   Mr. Billy Downs and His Likes

The title of *Mr. Billy Downs and His Likes* (Charles L. Webster and Company, 1892) was one that Johnston finally selected over such other possibilities as "Some Old-Time Georgians," "Old-Time Georgia Scenes," "A Bachelor's Counselings and Other Stories," "Mr. Billy Downs and His Contemporaries," and "Some Georgia Rural Folk."[24] As the tenth volume in Webster's Fiction, Fact, and Fancy Series, Johnston's collection of six tales found itself in the company of works by Mark Twain and Walt Whitman as well as Agnes Repplier, Irving Bacheller, and Poultney Bigelow. The author of this "tenth milestone," says Arthur Stedman in his "Editor's Note," is "the founder of a school of fiction and the dean of Southern men of letters," a man of "innate youthfulness" whose storytelling manner is "quite inimitable."[25] By now, however, the aging founder was beginning to imitate himself. Put more favorably, all of the stories of *Mr. Billy Downs* "are good examples of Johnston's art," exhibiting "familiar character types such as the bachelor, the widower, the spinster, young country people, and the shiftless backwoods farmer; conventional plot lines; and the familiar setting of Dukesborough."[26] There are here, again, a few effective deviations and noteworthy individualities, but its representativeness rather than its intrinsic merits best accounts for a reissuing of this book in 1900.

The title character Mr. Billy is the bachelor in "A Bachelor's Counselings," a shrewd assistant and finally himself a participant in felicitous matchmaking. Also, although it is combined less than perfectly with the account of a political campaign, the road to matrimony is obviously a central concern in "Almost a Wedding in Dooly District." Reminiscent of "The Pursuit of Mr. Adiel Slack" in

Dukesborough Tales, this tale has a fraudulent slickster named Putnam Davison whose villainy is fully if fortuitously disclosed at the end; here, however, it is Patsy Hammick, a fifteen-year-old girl of "weak understanding", who is deceived by Davison, while the old maid of the story, Emeline Lynch, is the admirable, clear-sighted guardian angel. The legal union of Patsy and Davison is prevented at the last minute, and, in further keeping with the happy-ending formula, Patsy makes a good later marriage.

"Something in a Name" and "The Townses and Their Cousins" focus more directly upon the state of matrimony, though they do so in very different ways. "Something in a Name" is the humorous story of the joining together of Phyllis Phips and Granville Quartley of Athens, Georgia. Once the husband has accepted his lot of clerking in his wife's millinery shop, a long life of marital bliss seems assured. Although the outcome of wifely triumph is the same, this little piece is as essentially unlike "Mr. Fortner's Marital Claims" as it is similar to "The Suicidal Tendencies of Mr. Ephrodtus Twilley." Like the Fortner story, "The Townses and Their Cousins" seriously explores the husband-wife relationship, but in its mood, in its picturing of malevolent greed and murder, in its study of the effects of guilt, it is like "The Pursuit of the Martyns." The marriages that Johnston opens to view are those of Joe and Mandy Willis, Tom and Sally Towns, and Ryal and Nancy Towns—the three husbands being, respectively, the witness, the victim, and the perpetrator of murder. Inherent in the plot are the legal devices of wills and courtroom cross-examination; the truth is revealed and right triumphs; the guilty or evil person succumbs contritely to death by some unexplained agency; and, as ever, and especially here, the goodness of women is contrasted to the fallen nature of men. Johnston makes specific authorial and legal comments on women's rights in this story, but more effectively he has the long-suffering Sally Towns observe before her husband's death, " 'The safest piece of meanness which a man can do in this world is meanness to his wife. The law gives him not only all her property, but the right to abuse her and slander her.' "[27]

Several familiar Dukesborough characters appear in "The Townses and Their Cousins"—the lawyers Mobley and Sandi[d]ge and the sheriff Mr. Triplett, for example. And by type and individual, Dukesborough residents appear also in the two other stories of *Mr. Billy Downs*. "Parting from Sailor" is another Mr. Pate story about big, mean Jim Rakestraw, who in this tale sinks so low as to put commercial value on a dog. In "Two Administrations" Johnston returns to the theme of education; Isaiah Cubbedge is a villainous schoolmaster who traffics in stolen property, and John Overby is a gentlemanly lawyer-turned-teacher who later and efficaciously institutes the Johnstonian honor system at the school. Including "Likes" in the title for this volume was an appropriate choice in more ways than one.

V   Little Ike Templin and Other Stories

Although a number of its tales were originally published in young people's magazines, *Little Ike Templin and Other Stories* (Lothrop Publishing Company, 1894) is perhaps not so much a book for children as it is a book about them. In any case, few of the readers of the thirteen stories, of whatever age and period, have found much to praise in this collection. The *Little Ike* tales, says one twentieth-century observer, have "little spontaneity and naturalness" and lack "local color and the subtle humor found in previous collections . . . . The pathos, which some of them attempt to express, seems rather superficial and forced."[28] Perhaps the juvenile slant is what makes the difference, but even Johnston devotees note here diminishing returns from his Middle Georgia stockpile. Plot is at a minimum, the sketching of an incident at a premium. A little Negro slave and a donkey are probably its most memorable characters.

The author of *Little Ike Templin* placed high value on literary pathos, as did appreciative reviewers whenever Johnston achieved his pleasing, peculiar blend of the humorous and the pathetic. Pathos is, however, the major and excessive ingredient in four of these stories. Two, "Oby Griffin" and "Poor Mr. Brown," faithfully present some local social conditions and practices, and are told largely through youthful Philemon Perch-like narrators. Little Oby, the title character of the first, is an eleven-year-old saintly invalid who receives baptism just before he is called to the heavenly home whence he so evidently came. Mr. Brown's halo, though posthumous and not quite so large because he is an adult, comes as a result of his attempt to repay the Templetons for the hospitality that they have for years freely and sympathetically given him as a traveler past their home. The pathetic didacticism so evident in these two tales is scarcely less obvious in "A Stepson's Recollection," another story with a fatal finale and, in Slemmer, a sickly carpenter, another exemplary, Christ-like figure. "The Two Woollys," although it pictures sentimentally the death of an angelic, precocious child, includes considerably more humor. By effectively focusing on Woolly Gear (the father) and not just upon

Woolly (the invalid son), this story comes close to being the touching and not the bathetic account of a father's loving relationship with his little boy. Johnston was much affected by the death of children, but several of his stories indicate he was too deeply moved to make effective literary use of his emotion.

In "The Two Woollys" Nimrod, a little hound puppy, is used to gain both humorous and pathetic effects. Animals figure in a large proportion of the *Ike Templin* tales, and in several of the sketches are central. "The Stress of Tobe," which reintroduces Mr. Bill Williams, now twenty-eight years old, and Philemon Perch, now a fifteen-year-old college student, is the account of a mule colt's mistaking an old horse named Tobe for its mother. The incident, probably actual and no doubt funnier for Johnston than he can make it for anyone else, is nevertheless more entertaining than the fight related in "Buck and Old Billy" between a confused billy goat and a ram. "Len Cane about Dogs" contains Mr. Pate's anecdotes of two of Len's experiences proving that "dogs is a heap smarter'n people gen'ly sispicions, and, more'n that, they has their langwidges on top of it."[29] "Careful Pleadings" is another dog story, but here Johnston is more concerned with people, some of whom, as he illustrates, are smarter than other people "sispicions." With the help of a little whiskey, the affable General Snow enables John Kilgore to forget all about his mission of shooting the General's dog for sheep-killing.

Lawson Wimpy, of whom Johnston paints an appealing but overdone domestic portrait, is the man who habitually outsmarts the bees in "The Bee Hunters," but like General Snow, Mr. Swint in "The Quick Recovery of Mr. Nathan Swint" and Jimmy Beazely in "Black Spirits and White" are the outsmarters of people. In order to get rid of "Buck," a maurauding bear being kept as a pet by a boy on a neighboring plantation, Mr. Swint feigns an illness that reportedly can be cured only by eating bear meat. And Jimmy Beazely, himself a youthful trickster, turns the tables on Tom Pullen as he tries to frighten Uncle Peter Burch, a free Negro who is a professed believer in ghosts.

Two stories that involve both juveniles and animals, "Little Ike Templin" and "The Campaign of Potiphar McCray" are the most noteworthy pieces of the collection. Although the familiar Johnston shortcoming of inadequately merging constituent incidents weakens this first tale, Johnston impressively displays here his forte of humorous characterization. The little Negro Ike, his mother Judy, brother Neel, and sister Till are memorable creations, their individual characterizations significantly enhanced by the interdependent family portrait that Johnston paints, a portrait that also includes their owner, the Widow Templin. The major incidents concern the ploys used to influence Little Ike, a cunning and devilish child who has a voracious appetite and who has refused until he is over two years old to walk or talk. The most amusing of the ploys is Neel's finally getting Ike to walk—indeed, getting him to run—by putting food in the napping brat's clothes and opening the gate for hungry Old Flop-ear the pig.

The basic situational conception and the authorial tone of "The Campaign of Potiphar McCray" do more to establish the success of that tale than does its characterization. The "campaign" which is chronicled is that of three barely teen-age Southern boys who set out to be the reinforcements to save the army of the Confederacy in the summer of 1864. It is, of course, a ludicrous and abortive adventure, well handled by Johnston in mock-heroic fashion. Contributing to Johnston's and, for a while, to the boys' and then finally to their parents' cause is Potiphar, the very vocal and independent mount of the expedition's leader. The youths' great enterprise is destined for failure when there is "an important desertion from the auxiliary force that was hastening to the relief of the army under General [Joseph E.] Johnston"[30]—when, in other words, the legendarily hungry, braying Pot gets over into an adjoining cornfield.

VI   Old Times in Middle Georgia

Other than the sixteen-story edition of *Dukesborough Tales* in 1883, no other collection of Johnston's short fiction contained as many as the fifteen tales of *Old Times in Middle Georgia* (The Macmillan Company, 1897). Johnston had to plead to secure reputable magazine publication for some of his last stories, and yet, even though everyone knew that his Middle Georgia vein was playing out, nearly everyone has found more to admire in this volume than they did in its predecessor. With *Old Times*, the second most unified of his volumes of short fiction, Johnston comes full circle. Though not rising to new heights, he rose to the finale, and his voice was unexpectedly strong.

Johnston's old fictional themes, concerns, and characters are all present in *Old Times in Middle Georgia*, just as all of them were in those old times their preserver loved so well. Six of the tales are old Mr. Pate's, which is an important unifying as well as an effective and appealing narrative device; and, according to its subtitle, one story is told by old Philemon Perch himself. Religious, educational, legal, moral, romantic: all of Johnston's humanistic local-color interests are represented. Nostalgic, humorous, pathetic, quaint, amusing, instructive—the book is, as a contemporary reviewer noted, an emotional rather than an intellectual one.[31]

With differing proportions of humor and pathos, a third of the tales of *Old Times* involve romantic interests and courtships. "Miss Clisby's Romance" and "Mr. Cummin's Relinquishment" are the more unusual and more serious of this group, which includes also "Old Lady Lazenberry," "Shadowy Foes," and "Their Cousin Lethy." "Mr. Pea Nearly Nonplussed" and "Mr. Pate's Only Infirmity" are character sketches of the two old gentlemen in the titles. Johnston reported himself very fond of Mr. Pate, and this latter tale can and did endear him to many readers as well. Told in retrospect by a favored and sympathetic auditor of Mr. Pate's, it is the story of the old man's revelation to his youthful friend of his reactions to increasing deafness. "Mutual Schoolmasters" is Johnston's pedagogical piece in *Old Times*. A story of informal self-education, it is short, didactic, and uninteresting. The legal story of the collection, with its concluding courtroom scene and its illustration of the shortcomings of the judiciary and of human nature, is "A Case of Spite."

Of the six remaining stories in *Old Times in Middle Georgia*, three are atypical, mediocre or worse pieces, and three are typical but significantly or fetchingly so. "Lost" is the five-page personal recalling of an incident that helps the narrator understand Christ's parable about the lost penny and the lost sheep, while "Ephe" and "Ishmael" are both stories about race. Ephe, in the pathetic tale that carries his name, is an eighteen-year-old free Negro who is rescued from the villainous hands of several other white men by Colin Duncan, whose son's life Ephe then later saves at the cost of his own. Set in the late 1860s in New York and Europe, "Ishmael" is scarcely recognizable as a Johnston production. Befriending his poor, unsuspecting half-brother, a tubercular consumptive who is the grandson of an octoroon leaves him an inheritance of $20,000.

"Mr. Eben Bull's Investments," "Our Witch," and "Weasels on a Debauch" come deep from the soil of Middle Georgia. The first of these is told by Philemon Perch and has some of the colorful interest and exuberant sparkle of which this nostalgic narrator had proven himself capable. Both Phil and Mr. Eben Bull learn a lesson about gambling after they confidently place a little money on Jack Withers in a footrace. Jack's country-boy opponent is Peeky Grizzle, whose "bowed legs looked like two long parentheses" but whose running "was flight. Yes sirs, flight!"[32] "Our Witch," told through the agency of Mr. Pate, shows how an old Baptist deacon is able to resolve the fantastic suspicions of Nancy Magraw regarding her neighbor Polly Boddy, whose only bewitchings are through her personal charm and unsurpassable mint juleps. More important, though, the characterization of Nancy and Andy Magraw is unusually serious and psychological for Johnston. His achievement in this effort is not that great, but the difference is noteworthy. "Weasels on a Debauch" is another Mr. Pate story about Len Cane's wisdom regarding animals. Building up an effective if low-key suspense, it is a good character sketch of Len which, with the tale's particular narrative method and its investigation of a domestic situation, also interestingly reveals other characters.

VII   Uncollected Stories

Although Johnston seems to have completed six short stories that were never printed,[33] only four of the tales he saw into print were never collected. Since only one, "A Challenge," appeared too late to be included in a collection, the exclusions of "A Term of Years Policy," "Man and Master," and "Edy Adkins" are undoubtedly deliberate.

Johnston's last published story, "A Challenge," appeared in the April, 1898, number of the *Century*. It is another humorous tale of Mr. Pate, whose story is reported by a more authorial persona. Wishing to show that he is capable of telling a fight story as well as love stories, Mr. Pate gives an account of the bluffing challenge to a "jule" [duel] which "Little Tony" Hopper issues through lawyer John Shannon to Tom Hatchett. Terrified by the idea of a duel and unable to comprehend the "dictionary" talk of Shannon, Hatchett contracts a raging fever and promises never to make Tony the butt of any more jokes.

"A Term of Years Policy" appeared in the May, 1894, *Catholic World*. Johnston could well have drawn on his own experience for this story of an honorable man and devoted husband and father who finds himself in rather deep debt, but the tale itself is sentimental and sermonic. Although Issac Kollock is talked out of his suicidal despondency by the good Baptist minister Brother Sanford, he manages nevertheless to expire only hours before the expiration of his $3,000 term-life insurance policy.

Though now almost entirely inaccessible, "Man and Master; or, On the Old Plantation" and "Edy Adkins: The Story of a Slave" are important inclusions for the Johnston canon. In each the central character is a sympathetically portrayed Negro slave, a character and a condition that Johnston, despite his antebellum Southern grounding, did not treat frequently in his fiction. Gilbert Brown is the faithful servant and beloved friend of his master for over fifty years in "Man and Master," which appeared in the August 23, 1884, number of *The Sunny South*. An honest, deeply religious man, "Uncle Gill" protects his master's interests and amuses the family with his biblical knowledge before, at the end, he joyously departs to the mansion of his Heavenly Master. "Edy Adkins," copyrighted in 1885 by the S.S. McClure Syndicate, was printed on August 4 of that year in *The* [Atlanta] *Weekly Constitution* and probably appeared elsewhere as well. With this story as with "Mr. Thomas Chivers's Boarder," Johnston proves that he did not blink at the cruel treatment sometimes given to slaves. Edy is violently whipped by the hateful Mrs. Sheals, the wife of an overseer who has hired out Edy from her owner, and when Mrs. Sheals is poisoned, the sullen Edy is convicted of the crime. She is, however, saved from execution in the nick of time through a chain of events that include her anguished husband's threatening of Mr. Sheals, Sheals's confession of the murder of his wife to the Reverend Mr. Sanford, and Sanford's procurement of an executive pardon for Edy.

VIII   *Johnston's Short Fiction: An Overview*

R. M. Johnston's nineteenth-century reputation and his twentieth-century niche in American literary history rest almost solely upon his short fiction. Of the sixty-seven stories and sketches that followed in time the sixteen of *Dukesborough Tales*, sixty-six echoed them in subject and form. Seen as a whole, these later pieces exhibit in language and in plot the growing professionalism of a local-color writer of limited range. Not all of the appealing genuineness, not all of the raconteur's natural vigor are lost, but for fiction whose primary objective value is pleasant amusement and historical preservation, the gain in sentiment and sophistication—and in repetitiousness—is not a compensatory advance. Always escape or entertainment fiction rather than significant interpretive literature, Johnston's tales and sketches became less and less entertaining.

Because such a natural whole, Johnston's short works have long been a single focal interest. Contemporary reviewers immediately saw each new collection of his tales in this context, and scholars who have had the complete canon available have recently made rather full analysis of it. Focusing on institutional or individual human activity, Leona Garner,[34] for example, groups all of Johnston's stories according to whether they deal with schools, lawyers and courts, religion, Negroes and slavery, or courtship. Jimmy Ponder Voyles's[35] enumeration of major subjects or themes—marriage, law, religion, education, and slavery—is identical to the Garner scheme, but, importantly, Voyles emphasizes that often two or more of these themes are combined in a single tale. Voyles has in addition a fifth category that he calls simply humorous stories and that he subdivides into stories about animals and stories with motifs taken from the Old Southwest humorists—such as muster day, athletic contests, the practical joke, the swindle, and physical discomfiture.

Clara Ruth Coleman Wood's[36] analysis of the canon is essentially formal or generic, but her categories also make much use of subject and, especially, character. According to Wood, among the twenty-four pieces of Johnston's short fiction that should be called *sketches* (simple descriptions of characters, the presentation of very brief action, or, even, some short essay-like productions), six have Mr. Joseph Pate as a narrator, four are exempla, four are animal stories, four tell of physically or mentally handicapped persons, and two are descriptions of people who have loved and lost. The fifty-four *tales* (short fiction that does not have the unity of a short story) may be grouped according to the recurrent characters who appear in them. Mr. Joseph Pate is involved in seven tales; Dr. Lewis, in four; Lawson Wimpy, in two; Bill Williams, in seven; and Philemon Perch, who, counting the tales in which he is involved with Mr. Pate or Bill Williams, appears in twenty-two. Sixteen other tales tell of Dukesborough citizens who, through repeated appearances, have become established residents of Johnston's fictional community: the lawyers Sandidge and Mobley, Sheriff Triplett, the preachers Mr. Sanford and Mr. Swinney, Deacon Leadbetter, Sally Burch, Betsy Wiggins, the Watts family, Jacob Spouter, and Josiah Cofield. Ms. Wood also recognizes that themes, plot situations, and character types as well as specific individuals reappear in Johnston's fiction. Professional or attitudinal types (the lazy and usually shifty character, the greedy villain, the denominational partisan, the schoolmaster, the justice of the peace, the slave, the old bachelor, the pretty widow) could, Wood believes, provide other large groupings, as could such recurrent "features" or "motifs" as Old Southwest humor, romantic tangles and misdirected courtships, or the efforts of lawyers to discover the truth and protect the innocent. Showing, among other things, that only five of Johnston's published tales make reference outside nineteenth-century antebellum Middle Georgia, Wood says setting could be the basis for yet another categorization.

A more technical analysis or classification of his short fiction moves toward evaluation of Johnston's literary achievement. In a study of the narrative method of four Georgia writers, Robert L. Phillips, Jr.[37] makes groupings according to the narrative situations that appear in Johnston's fiction. He discerns four: stories told by Philemon Perch concerning events that he himself either saw or participated in, stories told by Perch in which he pictures himself as listening to tales told by someone else, stories by an unnamed first-person narrator, and those told by an omniscient narrator. These different narrative methods are, however, as Phillips notes, only variations of a single situation: even though Johnston quit employing the name of Philemon Perch for a while, he never changed his basic narrative perspective of "an old man recalling his distant youth." So founded, all of Johnston's narrative methods, concludes Phillips, create "the impression of romance that comes from treating the typical and usual rather than treating the unique first-hand."[38] Moreover, because Johnston, who strongly felt the need for moral authority in his own life, believed strongly in the high didactic function of literature, "the obvious authority that [he] exercised over his characters, his insistence on his narrator's judgment, gives the stories a patent, formulaic quality that creates an artistically unacceptable romance."[39] Whatever, then, the stylistic achievements—the masterful dialect, the whimsical classical allusions, the authenticity born of attention to detail and careful description, the genial tone—the Johnston narrator is not only sentimental but, much worse, he gives the reader no choice but to agree with his sentimental evaluation. Johnston may have appreciated the individual worth of Middle Georgians more truly than their earlier chroniclers, but, as his narrative methods reveal, "the terms of [his] sensitivity cast doubt on the permanent value of his work."[40]

Revealing his methods of composition, Johnston plainly reveals what gives his short fiction its value as well as what detracts from it. Character and scene—superficially manifested, though in remarkable detail—are his fortes; plotting and the artistic unity of constituent elements are his weaknesses. In the *Autobiography* his writing procedures, or lack of them, are discussed at length:

In making up a story of imagination I never could do without places. I must see in my mind those places which I have seen with my eyes. My imagination, such as it has been, has taken care of the rest. In order to give greater verisimilitude to these stories, I sometimes introduced myself upon the scenes as taking part in their action. This was wholly imaginary, as well as most of the actions in the stories themselves. . . . Often when with intent to get up something new for a magazine, without a single idea or purpose in my mind, I have held my pen in hand for an hour or more, then laid it down, feeling that I had about gleaned all from my little field. But not content to turn myself away from the perspective [*sic*] of a check that for several sufficient reasons would be acceptable, I have turned my eyes again upon the past, and in time appeared before them yet another scene, whether in family life, in the village, courtroom, or elsewhere, as I began to revive it.

In the start I usually had only one or two characters in my mind, and none or little thought as to how long the story was to be conducted and how ended. As the subject revived in interest, other characters presented themselves, and according to my feeling the story went to five thousand, ten thousand, or twenty thousand words. Whenever it extended as far as the last figures, the manuscript, after the first writing, was wholly without unity, for during its writing other characters and scenes introduced changed entirely the current as it started forth. I seldom ended a story with the names I started with, for they also have always seemed important to my own satisfactory understanding and picturing of characters. Thus it happened very, very often, that an incident that I could have told in five minutes has developed into a story requiring one or two hours in the reading. As often has it occurred that a character selected for certain illustrations has evolved traits of which I had no thought at first, and varied far from the line which I had (but never very clearly) projected. Therefore, my custom has been to rewrite, seldom less than twice, frequently as many as four or five times. I could never feel that a story was finished until I could plainly see my characters and become thoroughly acquainted with their actions and the intent of their words. As for attempting to analyze them, I never felt that I had any sort or sign of gift for a matter that always seemed to me too subtle for me even to essay to study it. Recalling a scene of my boyhood or young manhood, and afterwards dwelling upon it with fondness, yet seldom without some sadness, I have put it into [*sic*] men, women, and children, often out and out inventions of my own imagining, yet in harmony, as I clearly remembered those whom I well knew in those periods. . . .

As for laying out in my mind plans for a story, I never once did or attempted it. That is a thing for which I never believed myself to have any capacity. Characters and scenes starting from one slight initiation in a place well remembered, have come along as my pen moved, and the *finale* became such as served to fit the actions. I always thought with my pen in my hand. . . .[41]

Here, stated at the source, is precisely what most critics have pronounced from the final products. Richard Malcolm Johnston created some memorable, if not significant and enduring, characters. In general, he faithfully and valuably reproduced the setting and life of Middle Georgia in the 1820s, '30s, and '40s. His pieces of short fiction can best be described as sketches or tales, for "even at his best he can hardly be classed as a short-story writer, certainly not if the definition is to be in terms of the French *conte*."[42]

Among the large body of short fiction that Johnston produced after 1883—fiction that might validly be called The Other Dukesborough Tales or The Other Georgia Sketches—are eight or ten stories that are capable of giving pleasure and are worthy of praise and preservation. Exactly which ones would be chosen might vary slightly from reader to reader, but a total of ten is not likely to be exceeded. Critical readers familiar with Johnston's works as well as the works of the Old Southwest humorists are less likely to agree with Carl Holliday's view of Johnston as "an example of steady, unremitting progress in literary excellence"[43] than they are with George M. Hyde's judgment in a comparative article in *The Bookman* in 1897. A. B. Longstreet's *Georgia Scenes*, said Hyde, marked the beginning of literary Realism in the United States and is "American humor writ large." R. M. Johnston's *Old Times in Middle Georgia*, on the other hand, "has the delicate aroma of old-fashioned roses, and must be classified with the blithe, ready-made fiction of but the day before yesterday (yet how distant!) wherein the raconteur aimed above all else to tell a 'good story,' the happy ending of which should be teasingly delayed till bright young eyes ask wistfully who married whom."[44]

CHAPTER 4

The Novels

F OUR of Richard Malcolm Johnston's works have usually been called novels, although he himself set the number at three and a knowledgeable scholar has set it at six, two long and four short ones.[1] All, more properly perhaps, are romances rather than novels. This chapter considers the usual four, those longer Johnston fictions that appeared as single, separate volumes. *Old Mark Langston: A Tale of Duke's Creek* (1884) and *Widow Guthrie* (1890) were published originally as books. The shorter *Ogeechee Cross-Firings* and *Pearce Amerson's Will* appeared first in periodicals, but were issued as separate volumes in 1889 and 1898 respectively.

In the early stages of their composition Johnston was pleased and excited about his novels, but he realized before very long that he was not a novelist. Set in Middle Georgia, these four longer pieces are like his short fictions in their local color, quite unlike them in their more serious intents and generally darker outlooks. Too much alike too many other undistinguished romances with their involved, overly manipulated plots, Johnston's long fiction affirms that the sketching of character was his prime literary skill.

I   Old Mark Langston

Encouraged in his first novel as he had been in his first professional story by his friend Sidney Lanier, Johnston saw *Old Mark Langston* announced by Harper's the same year that firm published the Franklin Square edition of *Dukesborough Tales*. Actual sales, at $1 a copy, began in January, 1884. The forty-two chapter, 338-page production is dedicated to the author's parents who, he says, made his "childhood so continuously blessed, that now, next to the solace of calling to mind persons and things that were then, is that of dreaming of some that were not."

Which characters and occurrences in *Old Mark Langston* "were"

90

and which ones "were not" cannot now be known with certainty, but for this work Johnston seems mostly to have drawn from dreams. If so, he dreamed long, for he worked on the book for three years, at times "laboriously."[2] Structurally, the novel is the slow unraveling of an old skein of crime and deceit. In it are the legal, religious, romantic, and educational Middle Georgia elements one expects from Johnston, and in it, hardly unexpectedly, the guilty are punished and the good and the long-suffering rewarded.

The book recounts the uncovering, after thirty years, of the illegal and immoral duplicity of Kinsey Duke, now the arrogant "ruler" of Dukesborough but earlier the pawn of his evil, avaricious father. Deserting a wife and child in Virginia in order to make the fraudulent claim of a runaway marriage to Emily Langston, he gained for the Dukes upon Emily's death the extensive property that she had inherited from Albert Semmes. Emily, who had in fact married Gerald Fitzgerald, bore twins, a boy and a girl, before she died a young widow. Her son, though unknown as such, is Lewis Sanders, a bachelor and a partner in a prosperous Dukesborough store. Lewis's twin sister is dead, but his niece Amanda, accompanied by the former Negro slave of her grandmother, is brought to Dukesborough by another uncle, Barney Jarrell (real name: Barney Jamison), who is the deserted son of Kinsey Duke. Full revelation is thus readied, and many are the residents of Dukesborough who help to effect or, especially, are affected by it.

Barney Jarrell is the prime mover, but two other persons instrumental in the disclosure are Lucius Woodbridge, a young lawyer-schoolmaster from Vermont, and Jesse Lines, the old justice of the peace who had married Gerald and Emily. Lucius's Catholic sister Rebecca, also a teacher, is able to marry Lewis Sanders once the truth is known, and Jesse Lines's daughter, Doolana, is wed to Barney at the end. Lucius also takes a bride, the cousin of a young man Amanda Jamison marries several years later. The saintly Mark Langston, Emily's father, and his quaint friend Baldwin (Baldy) Riddle, an elderly former admirer of Emily's, view the revelation of Duke's villainy and the ensuing marriages and their issues with special gratified interest. Mark's sister Mrs. Toliver, an ardent Baptist, and Mrs. Catlin, the only Methodist in Dukesborough, are other interested observers, the gratifying result in their case being that doctrinal wars become "more infrequent and less acrimonious," the truces "more prolonged and affectionate."

The weaknesses of *Old Mark Langston* are evident in even so simple a summary. While possessing the definitive qualities of the romance, by this time under heavy attack from the Realists, Johnston's book has few of the qualities of this genre at its best. The plot is complex and unexciting, and the characterization is merely two-dimensional. The book's morality is overly didactic, its sentimentality overbearing, and the striving and contriving toward these ends excessive and not always coherent. The covey of marriages which explodes in the last chapter may have been a concession to popular taste and fiscal necessity, but more likely it comes from the same deep source of personal taste as does the beatific invalid child who dies just after baptism and the repentant villain who, for his punishment, becomes "a whimpering, harmless imbecile."

The interest and value to be found in this first novel are relative, relative to Johnston's life and works and to elements within this work itself. For scholars and faithful readers of Johnston *Old Mark Langston's* description of Dukesborough is substantively important as well as stylistically and tonally representative:

Though Dukesborough was near three-quarters of a mile long, a brief description will serve for its topography. You understand it lost in width and populousness. The traveller, say he began at the beginning—namely, the cross-road—would see the meeting-house to the left and the graveyard to the right. Advancing in a direction westward, after ascending an easy acclivity, he would observe, on his right, at the corner of the graveyard, the blacksmith's shop, which at this period had so lengthened its lines and strengthened its stakes as to have an annex, in which spokes, hubs, felloes, and axle-trees were made from timber as good as the world ever saw. Keeping his eyes to the right, he would now pass in view, at convenient distances themselves apart, first Griffin's shoe-shop, in the rear of which Griffin himself dwelt in a house not much bigger than the shop; then the Duke mansion on the hill, one hundred and fifty yards from the street; then Barfield's. Right here the road, not having foreseen that it was to become a street, getting rather clumsily down the acclivity to its incipient level, diverged somewhat south-westwardly, and so continued until it concluded to fork, and thus define that limit of the town. Up to the fork, with liberal allowance for calf-pastures and truck-patches between, were Duggin's store and residence, Mrs. Catlin's, and the Howells', the last at the extreme west end. The said traveller, supposing his attention hitherto had been confined to objects of interest on his right, must right-about face, if his purpose were to do Dukesborough thoroughly and soon. Yet, pausing a moment at this point, he might observe, at short distance from the fork, one prong of which extended due west and the other south, another meeting-house, not nigh so large as the one aforementioned, and of another denomination of Christians. It had its little graveyard also. Beyond, an expanse of undulating country, covered with majestic growth, would invite him to penetrate. But, engaged with the investigation of Dukesborough, the tourist must take the back-track. A couple of hundreds of yards' walk would put him before Mason's residence, store, and post-office. Thence he would pass consecutively Mrs. Toliver's, Hallier's tavern, Barfield's grocery across the street from his mansion, Reuben Quillian's (opposite the Dukes'), and Colin Quillian's. Lingering, when a few rods beyond the latter, at the mouth of a lane that led due south, a moment's survey would show that it terminated at the academy grove, which was a mere extension of that around the church. Returned to the starting-point, he would now notice, if he had at first omitted, within the fork of the north and east roads, a small, clumsy-looking house, at present occupied by a new-comer.

It had been sometimes a disputed question whether this house, and the little church in the south-west fork, could fairly be regarded as being within the limits of Dukesborough. The lack of statutory enactments establishing definite corporate limits put off decision upon whether the occupant for the time being preferred to be considered townsman or countryman. For the south-west, Mrs. Catlin, the only Methodist in town, had often been heard to say that, as to whether her meeting-house was to be called a country or a town meeting-house, she was, and intended to remain, as independent as a wood-sawyer, so to speak; or, if people preferred a different comparison, a bob-tailed lizard; and that, as it would neither hurt the town for her meeting-house to be taken in, nor (especially) her meeting-house to be left out, she thought she might safely say for the latter that it was as independent as herself. Indeed, it is but fair to say that discussions upon the subject were held mainly at Barfield's, and the negative side maintained by country people, who, manifestly outside of the pale of town society, seemed to wish to confine that pale to its most narrowly ascertained limits.[3]

Since the Powelton, Georgia, of Johnston's youth is the acknowledged model for his Dukesborough, odds are that this discursive little tour provides an accurate picture of the real community. Johnston's fundamental dependence upon the literalness of his own experience is, in fact, especially striking in *Old Mark Langston*. Powelton, like Dukesborough, was famous for its academy, and the Vermonters, Lucian Whittle and Rebecca Pratt, who taught little Richard Johnston in Powelton cannot be unrelated to the Vermonters, Lucius and Rebecca Woodbridge, who preside over the Dukesborough school. Exhibiting another and even more personal relationship, Lucius is a lawyer-turned-schoolmaster who has to weigh the offer of a university professorship in Athens, while Rebecca is a Catholic who has to explain her religion to naive and misinformed, though good-hearted Georgia Protestants. The peculiar and specific

Georgia framework Johnston makes no attempt to disguise. He speaks factually of early nineteenth-century religious, legal, and educational leaders of Georgia—such men as Abraham Baldwin, Alonzo Church, the Beman brothers, Judge Dooly, and Jesse Mercer—and of such phenomena in Georgia political history as the famous Troup-Clarke factions.

A work whose ultimate value is historical rather than literary, *Old Mark Langston* does have some formal values—or at least some technical curiosities. Two of the chapters of this otherwise omniscient and authoritatively related romance, for example, are letters from Rebecca and Lucius Woodbridge to Vermont relatives. Welcome changes, these chapters show the appealing possibility of what a whole epistolary novel might have been. Another technical but more basic change had to do with Doolana Lines, widely admired and reportedly one of Johnston's favorite characters. "I started out to make Doolana mean and stingy, like her father," Johnston was quoted as saying, "but she wrenched herself out of my hands; 'I am a woman, and you shall not make me mean.' "[4]

Doolana Lines may have assumed such personal existence and had such strength for the chivalric Colonel; for readers of the novel she is, however, rather lifeless in comparison to her mean invalid father. Greedy, scheming old Jesse Lines is the most lively, appealing, and realistic character in the book, this in spite of his heavy dialect, his rapid Christian repentance, and his instant expiration, smiling into Doolana's face, upon revelation of Kinsey Duke's full villainy. It is as if his creator had to wrench Jesse from a burgeoning independent existence back into the romantic mold. Johnston's symbolism is too blatant in the chapter (XI) in which Jesse kills and captures flies as he converses with Kinsey Duke, but this, for Dick Johnston, is a most unusual foray into such subtleties. Whether Johnston realized it or not, Jesse Lines is one of the few of his characters who approach the three-dimensional.

Charles Forster Smith, an admiring acquaintance of Johnston's and an astute reader of his works, early recognized that while the old justice of the peace was doubtless not meant to be the strong point of *Old Mark Langston*, it was Jesse Lines who would "be remembered when all else in the book is forgotten." One reason the book would not be remembered, according to Smith, was its unbelievability: "It is not possible that a Georgia village could have been the scene of the unravelling of such a plot of avarice, meanness, cruelty, deceit, hypocrisy, lying, desertion, villainy—involving so many people in so many places, and extending over so long a period."[5]

A number of contemporary reviews of *Old Mark Langston* also charged improbability or absurd ingenuity, very few joining the *Hartford Post* in seeing the unusual plot and extraordinary working out of "details" as praiseworthy. While immediate critical reactions were divided over the virtues of Johnston's style, praise was generally issued for his humorous and pathetic effects, however. And while critics differed about the quality of his character sketches, or in some cases the native worth of the native models, there was little question about the historical and local-color value of his efforts in *Old Mark Langston*.

Most reviews found something to praise in spite of reservations, and some few reviewers praised without reserve. A century has not, however, confirmed Johnston's first novel as "a fresh study of human character and motive" which "must command attention." Neither the permanent value nor the above-average merit that were claimed for it in 1884 has become incontrovertibly clear. Today *Old Mark Langston* hardly seems "a genuine piece of literature" from a literary "artist"; assuredly, it has not today fulfilled the prophecy that it "will live and become popular."[6]

II   Ogeechee Cross-Firings

Johnston considered *Ogeechee Cross-Firings* simply a "story" rather than a novel, and it was, he recalled in his *Autobiography*, one of "quite a number" that he owed to the "timely suggestions" of his wife. First published in *Harper's New Monthly Magazine* in May, 1889, it appeared as a separate volume in Harper's Franklin Square Library in September of that year. For thirty-five cents a purchaser got not only Johnston's text but nine of its scenes as pictured by the highly regarded illustrator A. B. Frost.

The setting of the 149-page story is, of course, Middle Georgia, and its substance is local-color courtship. Three fatherless families—the Joyners, the Mays, and the Dosters—furnish the main players for this tale of the triumph of true love and true manhood. The two arrogant and rather profligate sons of the wealthier families, Hiram Joyner and William May, are expected to join these families with marriages to Harriet May and Ellen Joyner. Instead, Henry Doster and his cousin Tom make the conquests. Through a scheme to make the Joyners and the Mays, especially the brothers, believe that each cousin's interest is in the girl other than the one he truly desires, the gallant Tom and Henry each gain extravagant praise from the appropriate family and, ultimately, the lovely hand of the appropriate, approving young lady.

Although romantic love is clearly the central concern of *Ogeechee Cross-Firings*, an interrelated concern and the most important element of the book's local color is religion, specifically the Baptist-Methodist antagonism with which any reader of Johnston or any nineteenth-century native of Georgia was well acquainted. Here, as in *Old Mark Langston*, each denomination is embodied in specific characters, but in this instance the respective gospels are represented directly by ministers, the Reverends Allen Swinger and Henry Doster of the Methodist faith and the Reverend Mr. Bullington of the Baptist persuasion. Modeled upon Johnston's Hancock County neighbor and close friend, the widely revered Methodist bishop George Foster Pierce, Henry Doster is a "straight" man, a romantic lover-hero more than a typical rural American clergyman. Brothers Swinger and Bullington, on the other hand, are humorous, memorable constructs from the "remembered oddities" among "common acquaintances" that Johnston gave credit to his wife for helping him to remember.

Swinger and Bullington are the Johnston "originals" for this piece, the humorous, eccentric, "quaint" characters who helped to make Local Color literature with a capital L and capital C if not literature with a capital L. Each is an ardent advocate of marriage, Mr. Swinger for realistic reasons underlying very romantically stated ones and Mr. Bullington for the realistic if unstated reason that he gets paid for weddings. The names of these two would do justice to a comedy of humors. Brother Swinger had been a noted fighter in his youth and "had not left behind all of his native combativeness when he advanced upon a higher field." Along with his considerable advice on love and marriage, Swinger urges his protégé Henry to "make charges" upon his congregations, to come down out of the pulpit and march "right on *to*'em, right and left." While Brother Bullington does not, in this sense, so charge his auditors, he always looks as if he is about to: "Tall, like Mr. Swinger, but much heavier both in body and in spirit, gloomy-looking all the time, his brows grow darker at any thought of harm done or meditated against either himself or the religious faith of which for many years he had been a very bold, a very loud, and a reasonably acceptable public exponent."[7] The Reverend Bullington tried to laugh sometimes, but this was, reports Johnston, the humorist son of a converted Baptist preacher, an agonizing experience: "On such occasions the corners of his mouth would let down, his lower lip shrink and hide behind its superior, all making it appear that in him, among the various emotions of the human heart, that excited by humor was the most sorrowful."[8]

Young love was the emotion that excited the main characters and most interested the contemporary readers of *Ogeechee Cross-Firings*, but the generative loving nostalgia of its author must also have been an emotion of interest, an attraction that has superseded the other with the passage of time. Johnston's affectionate dedication of his story to Bishop Pierce is only the first of many direct evidences of his personal and longing look back, in this case more to the later "Rockby" years than to those of his youth. Nothing in the book is more valuable to the social historian, for example, than the long description of that famous Methodist frontier institution, the camp-meeting. And here the narrator is no even thinly disguised persona; he is patently and rather pathetically the exiled author himself:

When a man far away from such scenes, both in space and in years, begins to talk about them, he is prone to indulge too fondly. He cannot at least but love to muse, amid other recollections, on those long, so long ago camp-meeting days, and more on those camp-meeting nights. Religiously inclined, earnestly so, indeed, but not taking part in the exciting scenes which so many with varying purposes gathered there to witness, when the bugle would sound the call for silence and repose, when even all mourners' wailings would be hushed, it was a pleasant thing to take a rustic chair, and leaning against a post of the tent, sit and listen to the night music then rising in the woods, and dream and dream and dream of hopes and destinies for this life and the life eternal.[9]

III   Widow Guthrie

Published late in 1890 by D. Appleton and Company, *Widow Guthrie* is R. M. Johnston's second and last long novel. It is also his best one.

As early as the summer of 1887 Johnston was trying to find time, as he said, "to do some work on a purpose that I have been entertaining for some time of illustrating by a novel some phases of the most cultured society in Middle Georgia villages several years before the War."[10] Later, when he had completed his labors, he said that he had "been appealed to often" to picture the aristocracy and that "the Guthries" was his "answer."[11] Later, too, however, he more completely and accurately described the result as an attempt "to show some phases in the old-time aristocratic element in our Middle Georgia society, and its relations to the democratic."[12] The novel, about 87,000 words, was finished by early December, 1889. To Richard Watson Gilder, who was considering it for serial publication in *The Century*, Johnston reported that the story occupied "nearly a year of my most elaborate and my happiest work"[13]; to James Whitcomb Riley nearly a year later he said simply that he "worked on it tremenjuous hard."[14]

In what for Johnston is an unusually realistic rendering, *Widow Guthrie* chronicles the dissolution of the aristocratic Guthrie family of Clarke, Georgia, the death of the innocent Caroline Guthrie Stapleton preceding and helping to precipitate the retributive but absolving deaths of her less blameless brother and mother. Losing her beloved son Duncan and the last vestige of her sanity before relinquishing her own life, Hester Guthrie is rightly the title character of this novel, which justly has been called the story of how justice is brought to her for the mistreatment of her daughter. Mrs. Guthrie, always negatively disposed toward her daughter and extremely partial to her son, had long been suspected of fraudulent conduct with regard to her late husband's will. Even before the disapproved marriage to John Stapleton, Caroline Guthrie had not gotten what seemed a fair share of the estate of Alan Guthrie, who had loved his daughter dearly. No contest is made of this treatment or of the will until after Caroline's sudden death, when John Stapleton feels compelled to take action for the sake of his motherless children. A local attorney, the likable Thomas Tolly, and another promising young lawyer, Christopher Bond of Augusta, undertake the case for the manly Stapleton while honorable, widely known Seaborn Torrance is retained by Mrs. Guthrie. Bond also undertakes defense of the honor of Miss Sarah Jewell, to whom Duncan Guthrie has made overtures even though he is married to the finest of women. Bond is wounded by Guthrie in a duel, but Guthrie himself is soon mortally wounded in a provoked fight with Peterson Braddy, a long-time antagonist because of improper advances once made by Guthrie to Peterson's niece. Mrs. Guthrie witlessly expires in imagined reunion with her infant daughter, and it is left to Seaborn Torrance to interpret the widow's psychopathic history when the lawsuit is dismissed in court. John Stapleton's suit for the exemplary, long-suffering young widow Alice Guthrie is ultimately not dismissed, and all dark Guthrie shadows are lifted with this impending union.

In circumstances, events, and characters, *Widow Guthrie* has much in common with *Old Mark Langston*. Clarke, a county seat village of about five hundred inhabitants, is larger than Dukesborough, but like the little democratic hamlet and its environs, Clarke and its environs envelop the action of Johnston's second long novel. Just as the model for Dukesborough was Powelton, the Hancock county seat of Sparta is almost surely the model for Clarke. Revelation of an old wrongdoing by the community's leading—or at least wealthiest—citizen is the mainspring of each plot, and the respective outcomes, if not the respective revelations, are the same: loss of mental faculties and then death of the aristocratic sinner. (Those in complicity also die, and also die repentant.) Though pictured more fully in *Widow Guthrie*, the law and lawyers are important agents in both of these novels; Barney Jarrell and Lucius Woodbridge come almost instantly to mind when one reads the consultations between Tom Tolly and Christopher Bond. The character type who was Baldy Riddle in *Old Mark Langston* becomes Peterson Braddy in *Widow Guthrie*, and as the female New England school assistant in music, Sarah Jewell is the professional reincarnation of Rebecca Woodbridge. Both Sarah and Rebecca are matched with appropriately fine specimens of manhood, and in each case this pairing is only one of several, the conclusive reports of which brighten and lighten considerably what could be tales of much darker and heavier impact.

Evidence of the similarity of Johnston's two longest pieces of fiction is abundant, but there are, too, some noteworthy differences. The author himself called *Widow Guthrie* his most elaborate work, a designation that would seem mainly to refer to plot but that is most applicable in this case to characterization or, relatedly, to the central purpose of the book. A more complex, coincidental, or "elaborate" plot than that of *Old Mark Langston* is not easily found, and *Widow Guthrie* does not provide it. Certainly a reader's credulity is tested less sorely here than in the early novel. Structurally, though, *Widow Guthrie* has the innovative periodic placement of scenes of comic relief, the most comic of which depicts Marcus, Mrs. Guthrie's ostentatious Negro coachman. Too, Johnston's express intent of showing in some detail the relative conditions of aristocratic and democratic elements of Middle Georgia dictated more than simply a few scenes and a few characters, more even than his compulsive multiple matchmaking and extensive mining of personal experience might have provided ordinarily. However, the greater elaborateness seems dictated by a more serious intent, one expressed within the novel itself. When, as in the opening of Chapter XXXIII, an author reveals that his concern has been with "subjects of vital morality" and asserts that "much of the expiation of guilt is done by the innocent," the elaborateness of his work is likely to be, or should be, mostly in his characterization.

Just as the character of Jesse Lines is the most enduring and endearing feature of *Old Mark Langston*, the figure of Widow Guthrie most memorably dominates the novel that bears her name. The relationship between Duncan Guthrie and his wife Alice is presented with a forthrightness and subtlety seldom displayed by Johnston, but outside this individual context the achievement is not that great. Compared to the work of other, greater writers the characterization of Widow Guthrie also falls short; however, it does at least register on a wider critical scale, and it is unquestionably Johnston's deepest and finest penetration into psychological complexities. Far removed from his well-done character sketches in the mood and manner of the Old Southwest humorists, the picture Johnston paints of Mrs. Guthrie is stern and dark. Much of this harsh portrait is accomplished by authorial assertion, but much is accomplished—and all is corroborated—by the widow's actions.[15] More than usual, in other words, Johnston shows as well as tells. More than ever, as a result, he achieves a character of some solid human actuality.

Hester Pollard Guthrie, her creator states factually, was a proud and imperious woman—"untiring in energy, exacting of service from subordinates, a lender of moneys at the highest interest possible and a shaver of notes at the lowest, eager to restlessness for the accumulation of property."[16] Disappointed in love and resentfully considering her younger sister the victorious rival, she made a late marriage to fifty-year-old Alan Guthrie, who after fathering two children entered into a decline in which his "understanding dwindled faster than his physical being."[17] Mrs. Guthrie, who doubted the love of her husband and felt that her firstborn child cared nothing for her and everything for the father, confiscated the second child. With Duncan, the younger, she entered into a veritable if figurative Jocasta-Oedipus relationship, and to him she explained her early, deluded feelings about Caroline: "But I tell you, Duncan, it rankled through my very blood to think after all I'd been through in my life, and what I had been through for her, that she was the most beautiful thing I ever laid my eyes on, and then for her to not have any love for me!"[18] While she claimed not to have mistreated Caroline, she certainly did not treat her as she did Duncan, who is too selfish to urge any alteration in the maternal dispersement of family wealth. Her open hostility to Caroline's marriage to the good but insufficiently aristocratic John Stapleton abated only slightly after that accomplished fact. She ignored Caroline until it was too late, and the only consolation she could find for her daughter's death was in "increased hatred" for her son-in-law and "increased yearning for her son." "A temper irascible, sensitive, jealous, combative" in her youth had not been transformed for the better in her adulthood and old age.

In the limited intercourse that she has with other people, Mrs. Guthrie appropriately illustrates the qualities ascribed to her. The most telling scenes are those of the evening visits of Duncan Guthrie to his mother's house. Retiring to the piazza after supper on one of these occasions, she tells her son that she doesn't mind if his wife Alice visits the Stapletons occasionally "because it looks better before the community for some of the family to fall in there once in a while." And she goes on:

> Yes, light your cigar, my son. I don't mind it out here. Indeed, I love for *you* to smoke, although I despise the thing in the house when it's got cold. But I'd rather *you'd* smoke than not, because you love it, and because when other people are having you to themselves and I'm here all by myself, even the cold scent of your cigar, if nothing else, is some comfort to me, because it minds me of the times before anybody came between us; not that I don't think you married very well, and as well as any mother ought to expect. . . . Yes, smoke your cigar. I like to smell it when you are smoking. Nobody else. I hope Caroline, no matter how much *he* may want it done, will not name Jack Stapleton's child after me. [19]

Although her servants are devoted to her, Mrs. Guthrie's orders to her "maid" at the close of this evening make her imperiousness perfectly clear. "Judy," she says, "put your mattress on the floor at the foot of my bed, and when you've washed your hands, sprinkle some cologne water over both my pillows; then, after I get to bed, do you go to rubbing me till I get to sleep or tell you to stop." [20] A late-night revelation of plans shows both her scheming materialism and her inordinate love of her son. There is always some legal threat in the case of an independent woman, she says, and this is probably why widows are so willing to marry again:

> But that's neither here nor there to me that had as much of that sort of experience as I wanted, and the very idea of marrying again has always been to me—I'm simply speaking for myself—it's been nothing else but disgusting, as the very death! As a widow I have fought my way the best I could, and I'm ready to do it again. I know you are sleepy, and don't want to talk about business this time of night; but I just *had* to tell you something before I went to bed, and it's this. Duncan, you're mistaken if you think I haven't been preparing and keeping myself prepared for such as this; and I come to tell you. Half, at least half of the money that your father left and that I have made off the property is in this house, and is in metal. I've put some of it out at in-

terest; but I know how to shave notes and debts as well as anybody, and I'm going to gather it in and hide it along with the balance; and I'm going to put the land into money, and do the same with that.[21]

The only two situations to which the widow proves even initially unequal are the unexpected deaths of her children.

Widow Guthrie is as close as the chivalric Johnston ever came to a villainess—and to a realistic depiction of character. But because it was unusual, perhaps too penetrating and too "real," Johnston made pointed apology for it. Mrs. Guthrie, the wise Seaborn Torrance alone discerns, is insane. "Grandest woman I ever saw; but crazy," he concludes, "crazy as a bed-bug."[22] Later, in court, he publicly pronounces the fact and proceeds to explain the causes:

Ardently, intensely, passionately affectionate by nature, persuaded that from some members of her family the returns received were inadequate to what she lavished upon them, she had not strength to resist the impulsion which such a delusion imparts toward resentment that, with beings like hers, is perhaps the most grievous of misfortunes. It is the more grievous when the sufferer exaggerates both her own and the corresponding affections of others to whom she turns through the instinct of forefending absolute, abject despair. . . . To this infirmity it was easy for one admitted within her confidence to discover were attributable her strange neglect on one side, on the other her inordinate favoritism and the eager energy with which, in hope of holding on to the only love which she believed to be hers, she strove for the continuing accumulation of what, estimating by a standard too often true, she regarded most contributory to that end. In the case wherein to outsiders her natural affection seemed to have been obtunded, its very intensity was the source of its disappointment.[23]

The absolution of Widow Guthrie has been preceded by that of Peterson Braddy and is immediately followed by an absolution of Duncan pronounced "with much feeling" by Christopher Bond. Absolutions complete, there remain only the usual reports of marriages to round out the story. Precisely because such artificially restorative elements are present, however, *Widow Guthrie* is not a satisfyingly completed piece. What had the potential to be a significant glimpse at the human condition in a Middle Georgia manifestation is ultimately an insignificant run-of-the-mill romance. Overpopulated and ill-proportioned, *Widow Guthrie* gives little esthetic pleasure. Its author's compulsions for multiple love matches, for moral didacticism and happily harmonious endings, for nostalgic reminiscences and an expository abundance of local color result once again in an unsatisfactory whole, an incoherence that is finally the hallmark of Johnston's longer fiction.

While *Widow Guthrie* cannot be called a good novel, Johnston's hopes that it would be considered his best work were not entirely forlorn. The book got favorable contemporary reviews and was probably the best-selling work he ever published. One reviewer called it a "strikingly realistic" work, and the bold, "admirably drawn" figure of Widow Guthrie—"a figure curiously compounded of cynical hardness, blind love, and broken-hearted pathos"—was widely recognized as the book's central achievement. Other contemporary praise is today more open to question. The novel hardly seems "carefully written" or "decidedly strong, well sustained, and of unfailing interest." The duel between Duncan Guthrie and Christopher Bond and the slaying of Duncan by Peterson Braddy hardly seem "descriptive masterpieces." That this oedipal story—a story of psychopathic evil, selfish near-adultery, and handgun homicide—could be called "one of the happiest, sweetest, quaintest novels that have come from the press in a long time"[24] is not so surprising, however. That there are grounds for such an interpretation is a major clue to Johnston's failures in *Widow Guthrie*.

IV   Pearce Amerson's Will

Another contested will, this time a truly fraudulent one, is the predictable propellant of Johnston's last novel. Dedicated to "the Old Bar of Georgia," *Pearce Amerson's Will* appeared first in *Lippincott's Magazine* in December, 1892, and was published in book form by Way and Williams of Chicago in 1898. "The favor accorded to this book in its [initial] appearance . . . ," Johnston wrote to readers, "seemed to justify its republication in this form."

Wiley and Cullen Amerson, the two sons of Pearce Amerson, are two very different men, as their respective marriages suggest. Wiley, the older brother and the villain of the piece, married Julia Marston for reasons of wealth and social status, while Cullen made a lower connection but a pure love match with the innocent and lovely Hannah Enlow. Talking against his younger brother, whom he has always resented, Wiley persuades his father to make out a will much to Cullen's detriment and greatly to his own advantage. When Pearce Amerson sees the truth and wishes to destroy the will, Wiley provides him with what he believes is a copy and not the original document. At

Pearce's death, then, Wiley is the major beneficiary under what is erroneously accepted as his father's authentic last will and testament. As if the double deception of his father and the shameless treatment of his wife were not enough to establish his evilness, Wiley attempts to make love to his beautiful sister-in-law, a passionate pursuit that he continues publicly after the deaths of Julia and Cullen. Hannah's former suitor, the stalwart young lawyer Arthur Dabney, and the sagacious solicitor Seaborn Torrance then move in as the investigative agents of justice to expose Wiley's villainy. Wiley is finally found dead after he has run away and lived in seclusion for several months, and Hannah is happily wed to Arthur Dabney.

Pearce Amerson's Will bears, in substance and in shortcomings, as great and obvious a similarity to *Widow Guthrie* as the latter does to *Old Mark Langston*. Johnston's interest is again in "subjects of vital morality," and again his solution to the problem of either inherent or psychopathic evil is a nonlegal solution achieved through lawyers. Again, too, the insanity and death of the villain are accompanied by a marriage involving at least one of the long-suffering wronged. While, as some readers have felt, irrelevant authorial comments and moral preachments are not as pronounced in *Pearce Amerson's Will* as in *Widow Guthrie*, the didactic authorial presence is still strong. *Pearce Amerson's Will* is, to be sure, the most melodramatic of all of Johnston's long fictions. It becomes almost an exemplum through the speech delivered by Seaborn Torrance.[25] "As you know," says Torrance, who probably is modeled upon Alexander H. Stephens, "I'm not a church member, but I'm not more sure of my own existence than that this world is governed by an Intelligence which is as good and merciful as it is wise, which, in cases like this of the widow and child of a good man, uncovers rascality for the purpose of beginning its punishment here, right here, knowing that it won't do to put it off."[26] Yet, devilish wretch that Wiley Amerson is, says the lawyer, he "deserves compassion, and he has mine most sincerely."[27]

About Augustus (Gus) Rachels, the local tavern keeper, Seaborn Torrance has other feelings: "The older I get, the more I admire how it is that the good Lord often puts in lowly places men such as him."[28] Such may legitimately be considered the basic feeling of Johnston himself, and this opinion is clearly manifested in *Pearce Amerson's Will*, as in all other of his works. The most-developed characters from among the lower ranks of society are Gus, Owen Carruthers, and Mr. Elisha (Uncle Lishy) Flint; and these characters, although they do not become three-dimensional, are much more alive than the aristocratic cardboard figures they interact with. Alcohol, dispensed by Gus and heartily consumed by the other two, is one internal explanation of their animation, but, more fundamentally, especially in the characterization of Uncle Lishy, Johnston displays the droll humor and appealing quaintness for which he had a reputation. Lishy Flint, for example, has several personal rules that guide his drinking and prevent overindulgence. One is never to take a drink when he wants it really bad: "Many time somethin' happen and my jaws gits to a waterin' and a solid achin' for a dram, then I clamp 'em together tight, and I says to 'em, 'No jaws, you want it too serwigous. . . .' "[29] Another principle is always to eat a biscuit after having a little toddy. The good and expected benefits of whiskey come only, he testifies, by putting a little something "on top of her where she went."[30]

That this same Elisha Flint is made to carry a proposal of marriage from Willey to Hannah is splendid microcosmic instance of how and how far Johnston goes wrong in this novel. As in *Widow Guthrie*, some less pleasant and less moral facts of human nature are recognized but are not realistically or honestly handled. If, for instance, marital infidelity had not been introduced deliberately into the story, Johnston's substitution of pious platitudes, sentimental deathbed scenes, and quaint humor for serious consideration of this subject would not be so noticeable. That troubled marriages are authorially and assertively interpreted rather than being opened more naturally to the reader's view is, again, ultimately unsatisfying. A modern reader welcomes the romantic Johnston's recognition that such marriages exist, but he earnestly wishes for something less than sainthood or satanism on the part of one spouse or the other.

There can be little doubt on the evidence of *Pearce Amerson's Will* that Johnston saw the highest purpose of literature as affectingly and didactically moral. He himself could get so wrapped up in the characters he had created that, as in the case of this last novel, his eyes would fill with tears when he looked at engravings illustrating the work.[31] He regarded a writer as the Providence of his characters, and God, he has Julia Amerson say, "regards with particular watchfulness the things done to widowhood and orphanage."[32] Had Johnston's watchfulness been less sentimental and less conventional in this last novel, something other than its local color might have significance today.

V   *"I doubt him on a long novel. . . ."*

As was true for the local colorists in general, Richard Malcolm Johnston's novels fall short of his achievements in the short tales and sketches. Several factors, some common and some unique, conspired toward this end.

Even with his short productions, Johnston was more "a writer of humorous sketches . . . than a creator of artistically constructed short stories."[33] Not surprisingly, he said he found it harder to write short pieces than to write long ones;[34] the conciseness that he saw as the secret of success for good writing he himself never mastered. For Johnston, character was supreme, and the starting point of all of his literary productions was either a character or an illustrative incident. That, as he claimed, he never made a careful advance plan for any of his stories is manifest to an extreme in the novels. What he always did essentially in all his fiction was simply to remember, and one remembers in sharp little images and vignettes, not in unified, well-integrated plots.

The autobiographical and nostalgic elements of his fiction are especially important in a consideration of Johnston's novels. Darker in outlook, more honest in some of their recognitions, more somber in tone than his lighter short works, his longer fictions never become too dark or too somber or perfectly honest, either. The veil of difficult intervening years was insurance against it: "To those survivors among the associates of my youth," reads the dedication to *Widow Guthrie*, "to whom, as to me, the old Georgia seems to have been more happy than the new." In addition, Johnston's literary taste, developed during those antebellum years in Georgia, lent its support to happiness and to the form and attitude of the romance. For one whose early reading included Issac Mitchell's *Alonzo and Melissa*, Louisa Sidney Stanhope's *The Bandit's Bride*, George Walker's *The Three Spaniards*, and Jane Porter's *The Scottish Chiefs* and *Thaddeus of Warsaw*, Johnston's four novels are predictable productions in more ways than one.

His inventiveness minimal, Johnston could not satisfactorily sustain a long narrative. Struggling, he moved to easy technical solutions and obvious vehicles for melodramatic moral instruction. All too evident to late twentieth-century readers, the shortcomings of the novels did not pass unnoticed by earlier readers. In Johnston's more complicated stories, noted W. A. Webb, "the plots are often artificial and the denouement is apt to be unsatisfactory." Moreover, says Webb, Johnston's villains, while "never quite consistent" individually, have collectively "a rather monotonous trick . . . of escaping the consequences of their evil deeds by becoming helpless imbeciles or harmless idiots when their rascalities are discovered."[35] Malcolm

Johnston "has no equal in his short stories, in humor and in character," Charles Dudley Warner wrote to Grace King in 1890. But, said Warner, "I doubt him on a long novel."[36]

CHAPTER 5

The Nonfiction

ALTHOUGH Johnston knew well and gratefully that his local-color stories were his meal ticket, he came to view his work in this "line" with self-deprecation and even embarrassment. He had become a writer of fiction "partly by accident," he reported to William Malone Baskervill in 1897, the most important reason being "that I had to make a living for myself and my large family *some how*." Expressing, in this same letter, appreciation for favorable reviews of *Old Times in Middle Georgia*, he told Baskervill, "I shall write no more stories, and am thankful to have made so reputable a retreat."[1] Nine years earlier, his reputation on his mind, he had written poignantly to E. C. Stedman that he did not want to be remembered "only as an aged clown."[2]

To one who spoke of "mere story-telling" and who considered "the production of beneficent results" the highest purpose of literary pursuits,[3] sportive fiction was a barely tolerated literary product. Fiction was a genre infinitely below poetry anyway, and humor was a mode far inferior to pathos. A gentleman-scholar devoted his time to *serious* writing: to drama or to poetry if he wrote inspiredly; to literary criticism, history, biography, philosophy, or perhaps even travel or the personal essay if he were less ethereal.

Johnston espoused such ideas more passionately as he neared the end of his life, but he had long held these beliefs. Not adverse to trying to earn a little money with serious productions, he looked more to posterity and to personal satisfaction than to profit with these "earnest" endeavors. The quantity of his published nonfiction is large; its literary or scholarly significance, small. Although his hope of becoming a recognized poet was not realized, he did achieve national publication and some recognition as a biographer, travel writer, literary historian, critic, and general essayist on matters literary, social, historical, religious, and personal. "Acumen and enthusiasm" he displayed on occasion,[4] but there is little of distinction to be found in these thousands of printed pages. Seen as a large whole, Johnston's nonfiction is—to put it as euphemistically as possible—"a realm where others are his peers."[5]

I   "... a thing of God"

Although Johnston is known to have written only two poems, one of which was never published, no biographical-critical study of this man can omit mention of his poetic endeavors. "Wind of the Winter Night" appeared in the *Southern Magazine* in March, 1874. "I Dreamed that I Had Dreamed" remains in manuscript, left among Johnston's papers at his death.

Writing to Alexander Stephens in the sportive dialect correspondence once carried on between them, Johnston lamented "the bizzy skenes of a vane an phoolish world" which prevented him from producing more poetry, from achieving his "lofty yit honest ambishion" of being a poet.[6] In this discussion of writing "oads," Johnston was, of course, being frivolous, but his silly confession of 1863 takes on a serious and even sad irony in the perspective of the remaining thirty-five years of his life. Poems, he believed, have "always [been] our best literature."[7] Philip James Bailey in the "Proem" to *Festus* had seen poetry as "a thing of God," and Johnston, a devout man who knew *Festus* well, would have agreed. Unquestionably he longed, and he long strove, to create this thing.

His single published poem is the more lyrical and by far the shorter of the two extant productions. The fourteen-stanza, seventy-line, iambic pentameter "Wind of the Winter Night" is a reflective piece about the dead. Although it is heavy with biblical and classical allusions, some readers have understandably been reminded of the poems of such pre-Romantics as Parnell, Black, and Young.[8] Shelley's "To Night" has been suggested as the specific model,[9] but the similarities are not overwhelming. Almost three times as long and with a differing, much more regular meter and rhyme scheme, Johnston's poem is also quite different in tone and theme. More melancholy, it conveys almost disconsolateness along with its scholarship. Certainly it does not have the comparative artistic naturalness or peaceful power of its supposed precursor.

Less poetic merit if more intrinsic and biographical interest are offered by the narrative "I Dreamed that I Had Dreamed." This long (seventy-six stanza, 570-line) poem tells of the glorious reunion of two lovers, Wilfrid and Genevieve; betrayed by Wilfrid's groomsman, Rudolph, the two have remained separated and in ignorant misunderstanding, though lovingly faithful, until a heavenly dream precipitates a reconciliation after nearly twenty years. The last stanza may serve to give an adequate taste of the whole of "this lover's tale":

> Bravest among the brave the man, and he
> Alone, may thankful thus appropriate
> The sorest trials of adversity,
> The pains of mankind young as trifles rate,
> Which nought from life's ideal good abate,
> As dreams remembered fond, and fondly told
> In tranquil time of ripened age and old.

What is most important about this extensively reworked and variously titled manuscript poem is that it represents for Johnston a futile literary pursuit of over thirty years' duration. When he wrote in February, 1874, to tell Alexander Stephens of the publication "of some lines from me on the Wind of the Winter Night," he told him also, "I have a longer poem which I will show you some day."[10] Nearly a year later he informed Stephens, "I have at last finished my poem on which I have been working off and on for over ten years."[11] Soliciting opinions on the work from such local friends as S. T. Wallis and no doubt Sidney Lanier in the 1870s, he turned to new literary friends in the North during the next two decades. J. C. Derby's comments and influential aid he asked for in 1884, E. C. Stedman's in 1888, and A. B. Frost's in 1889. Of the tactfully lukewarm responses, Stedman's is the fullest and most tactful. Johnston's idyll, Stedman wrote him, is clearly the work of a poet, but it is imitative and undistinguished; the characterization is not very effective and the narrative not very dramatic. He advised the poet-supplicant to leave well enough alone and stick to writing his local-color sketches. In these, said Stedman, Johnston "does *better than any one* else," and they are "in a *manner created by yourself alone*—and therefore unrivalled."[12] Although an aging Johnston forecast his satisfaction if only his "verses" could achieve publication and be "received 'respectfully,' "[13] their publication was consistently, respectfully, and discriminatingly denied him. The personal dream, unlike the narrative one, did not ever come true.

II *Professorial Preferences*

Except when he was being addressed in conversation, Johnston once wrote Alexander Stephens, he preferred being called "Professor" rather than "Colonel."[14] The academic, professorial tendencies of the man were, in fact, pronounced. His first book, *The English Classics*, and his next to last, *Lectures on Literature*, are works of literary history and criticism, and in between came many periodical articles of these types. E. C. Stedman, who had told Johnston that he had "a genius rarer than that of any critic,"[15] well might have added that his genius was not criticism. But this the scholarly Professor already knew. "I am not much of a critic," he modestly but accurately told Madison Cawein, "particularly of verse. . . ."[16] What Johnston had to say about literature is ultimately more significant for what it reveals about him than for what it says about the various writers who were his subjects.

To make such an assessment should not, however, obliterate the contemporary value and the important purposes that some of Professor Johnston's academic publication served. While neither his University of Georgia course in English literature nor his textbook was a "first," the two come early enough in the history of teaching British literature in American universities to make Johnston a recognizable pioneer in the field, especially in the South. J. B. Lippincott and Company of Philadelphia had enough confidence in him to publish in 1860 *The English Classics: A Historical Sketch of the Literature of England from the Earliest Times to the Accession of King George III.* Johnston's preface calls the work a "cursory account," and that label along with the "sketch" of the subtitle are not inappropriate. The attempt to cover too much chronological time may have handicapped the work, but its superficial breadth and its lack of specificity, even of dates, are notable. Among other shortcomings are a confusing organization (Chapters 1 - 12 are arranged by historical chronology, Chapters 13 - 24 by literary genre), the intrusive insertion of comments on religion, an almost exclusively moral basis of critical evaluation, and an excessive reliance on a few secondary sources.[17] Although a friend in Athens praised the author's "taste and judgment"[18] and Lippincott's reported that most early notices were complimentary,[19] *The English Classics* did not prove an academic or financial success. Ten years later, in 1870, the professor was offering to purchase copies that his publishers still had in stock.[20]

To Johnston if not to Lippincott's, however, the book or the idea was successful enough to justify an "expanded" version. Johnston's complimentary friend in Athens, the Reverend Stephen Elliott, had in 1860 urged a second edition, one which would be more like a German handbook. The new edition, though not Elliott's suggested format, was finally realized in 1872: *English Literature: A Historical Sketch of*

English Literature From the Earliest Times, a collaborative production by Johnston and his Baltimore friend William Hand Browne. For
this book, published by the University Publishing Company of New
York and Baltimore, Johnston made some revisions and slightly extended the eighteenth-century coverage of his original text while
Browne covered the literature from that point to the present. It was
thus Browne who was mainly responsible for what was new, who, as
Johnston noted, did "the most of that from what I have already
written."[21] The coauthors saw their book as a "manual" which
attempted, as they said in the preface, to give a "just idea of English
literature as a connected whole—an almost unbroken stream flowing
through English history, influenced by it, and in turn reacting upon it,
as a river cuts and shapes the valley which gives it existence and deter-
mines its course—at every epoch showing its connection with the
historical past, its intimate association with all contemporary events,
and even, by anticipation, reaching forward into the future."

The two compilers go on in the Preface of *English Literature* to
forswear any claims of originality either in the design or execution of
their production. "They . . . freely availed themselves," they say, "of
whatever suited their purpose, in the best critical and historical
writers to whom they had access." This admission made, this text does
not include, as had its predecessor, specific bibliographic footnotes
nor a final List of Books Quoted and Referred To. It does have,
however, the added features of representative literary selections and
lists of authors not covered in the text, and, as Jimmy Ponder Voyles
points out in noting the altered treatments of Milton and Marlowe,
Johnston's pronouncements now seem a little less offensively
authoritative and unqualified.[22] The professor's critical judgments
are still religiously and morally grounded, however, and the factual
inaccuracies that occur testify to the uncritical use of readily available
secondary sources. *The Baltimore Bulletin* was, nevertheless, very
high on "this very clever joint production of our genial humorist and
our subtlest critic."[23] Finding it excellent reading as well as a fine
guide to wholesome literature and a storehouse of exemplary
criticism, the *Bulletin* reviewer believed *English Literature* a good
book for the boudoir as well as the library. Today, even though it went
through several printings, the book may be found, in profound
repose, in only a few major libraries.

One writer on whose achievement the compilers disagreed was
Charles Dickens, a favorite of Johnston's. His reactions to this English
novelist reveal much about his own predilections and his own

achievements in fiction. In Dickens, as in Shakespeare, both the subjects of several Johnston articles, he admired especially the
characterizations and the artistic "intermingling" of the "serious and
the sportive," a combination that he himself was never able to achieve
artistically. Another of his articles, "George Eliot's Married People,"
might be assumed to shed some light on Johnston's own work, itself so
fecund in married or to-be-married folk. More light is shed, however,
on the essentially biographical and ethical tenets of his criticism, as a
single sentence from this piece will illustrate: "Aside from gratitude
for her almost matchless creations, we must be touched by the con-
templation of what must have been the sadness of a woman who did
not believe that happiness was to be had in married life, who had no
experience of happiness without, and who, although without ascertained principles of religious faith, and with an ineffaceable blot upon
her own life, yet shrank from imparting precepts which might lead
others to ruin."[24]

Johnston believed that "the faculty of composing interesting con-
cretes, whether in verse or in prose, out of the discordant elements of
this lower life was bestowed by the Almighty for benign purposes."[25]
This is how he approached and evaluated all literature, and in the
Catholic periodicals *The Rosary* and *The Catholic World* he was
allowed and probably encouraged to bring both Continental and
English writers under this particular focus. "Irish Lyric Poetry,"
"The Minnesinger and Meistersinger," "Modern German Religious
Poets," "A Poet of the Reformation," "Some German Catholic
Poets," "Some Polish Poets," "Sir William Davenant," "Alexander
Pope," "John Dryden," and "The Extremity of Satire" (Thackeray)
all saw publication in these two periodicals in the 1880s and '90s.

Professor Johnston's last academic volume, *Lectures on Literature:
English, French and Spanish,* also had both Catholic impetuses and
the auspices of Catholic publication. Appearing in 1897 in the
Catholic Summer and Winter School Library series published by D.
H. McBride and Company of Akron, Ohio, it is the culmination of a
lifetime of lecturing about literature. According to the preface, the
lectures are some of those that Johnston had delivered in the various
series which he conducted at the Convent of Notre Dame and at the
Peabody Institute in Baltimore, but some had probably also been
given as part of the popular professor's (and famous convert's) lectures at the Catholic Summer Schools at New London, Connecticut;
Madison, Wisconsin; and especially Plattsburgh, New York. The lectures, as orally presented and as collected in print, says Johnston, are

"intended mainly for those who have leisure for cursory, rather than prolonged and critical study of the matters herein discussed." "Cursory," it may be recalled, had also been Johnston's adjectival choice in the preface to his *English Classics* thirty-seven years earlier.

As the subtitle indicates, consideration is given to at least some aspects of three national literatures in this volume, the amount of consideration decreasing as one proceeds from England to France to Spain in the respective three sections of the book. Once again, what the critical judgments and historical selectivity reveal are more interesting and important for elucidating Richard Malcolm Johnston than for appreciating, say, Beaumont and Fletcher, Montaigne, or Lope de Vega. In his discussion of English drama, for example, Johnston asserts that suffering is a great blessing and argues the close and necessary basic connection of mirth and grief, of the sportive and the serious, of the humorous and the pathetic. A concern with verisimilitude and with depiction of the life of the common man in literature is reflected both in this first section and elsewhere. Similarly evident, however, are Johnston's convictions of the high and pure estate of womanhood and the belief that the poet "must not exhibit human nature in all its repulsive nakedness," that "the most heart-rending and dreadful pictures must still be invested with beauty and imbued with a dignity higher than the common reality."[26] Although it reflects too much Johnston's own brand of biographical criticism, it is difficult not to read a certain personal wistfulness into his statement about Don Pedro Calderon which closes the book: "Never were both patriotism and religion more loyally and ably represented than by this poet, who had the happiness to live in the most glorious period of his country's renown, and then to depart before its close."[27]

III   "*. . . running observations upon several subjects*"

Besides his critical articles on literature and literary figures, Richard Malcolm Johnston wrote a variety of other short prose pieces that gained national publication. Twenty of his essays, including some literary ones, were collected in two small volumes published by the Bowen-Merrill Company in 1891 and 1892. To James Whitcomb Riley, who was assisting him in the drawn-out negotiations with the publishers, Johnston issued several reminders that many of his essays which had appeared in magazines and reviews had received very high praise and commendation.[28] And although, he said, he knew that collections of essays did not sell extremely well, he immediately began to think about additional collections when his first became a reality. "If that goes well," he told Riley, "I may put out more of the same sort, as I have more than five times as much other material of the same sort."[29]

Like many of his literary articles, many of Johnston's other printed articles were originally prepared as lectures or addresses. From his young manhood Johnston had been in demand as a speaker at special institutional events, and he early saw many of these effusions put into print. The practice was one that spanned his whole adult life, from an "Address on Female Education" in 1856 to the "Address Spoken at the Georgia Academy of the Blind, June 27, 1867" to an oration on "The Dead of Georgia" at the 1869 commencement of the University of Georgia to an address on "School and College Discipline" before the Philomathean Society of St. John's College in Annapolis in 1873 to a speech to the New England Society in New York in 1896 to an address on "The Planter of the Old South" before the Southern History Association which was printed in that society's first volume of *Publications* in 1897. These particular examples are ostensibly direct reportings of the speech, but many presentations originally delivered orally were reworked for later publication. Some essays were, of course, written expressly for the medium of print, however. These two genetic types Johnston recognized through specific acknowledgments in the preface to the first Bowen-Merrill volume, and here, too, he made a specific apologetic characterization which covered considerably more than the essays in this volume. This collection, he wrote,

has been made partly out of selections from a series of Class Lectures at the Peabody Institute, in Baltimore, and partly from articles contributed to several American Reviews during the last twenty years. Written in the intervals of business engrossments, they lay no claim to very earnest thoughtfulness, but are mere running observations upon several subjects of literary and social interest, and are submitted to the public with whatever degree of modesty may be regarded consistent with such submission at all.

While *Studies, Literary and Social* (First and Second Series) was the title that finally graced the Bowen-Merrill volumes, the author's own earlier designation had been "Essays, Historical and Literary."[30] These respective nouns and adjectives provide, if not an exhaustive, an ample and enlightening description of all of Johnston's short nonfiction prose. Clearly, many of his articles are historical as distinguished from literary in nature, and again in this type the expository, the competent but not especially incisive, professor is often evident. Again, too, in many cases, the professor's deep moral orientation and, especially, his denominational religion are in evidence. While he published articles on Belisarius and Benjamin D'Israeli [sic] in *The Southern Review*, for example, he later wrote on Thomas More, Anne Katherine Emmerich and Clement Brentano, Roger Bacon, Adelaide Anne Proctor, St. Colomba, "Edward Hyde's Daughter," and "The Royal Patroness of Columbus" for *The Rosary, The Catholic World*, and *The American Catholic Quarterly Review*. Only one anomalous strict historical reporting job seems to have been undertaken as disinterested hack work: the contribution he made to Scharf and Wescott's *History of Philadelphia, 1609 - 1884*.

The "historical" and "social" labels are not necessarily mutually exclusive, but the more general "social" tag seems most appropriate for such Johnston pieces as "Celebrated and Common Friendships," "Pre-American Philosophy," "American Philosophy," "The Legal Profession," and "The Schoolmaster." These last two, though on the subject of two of Johnston's own choices of profession, remain general and objectively expository rather than personal and revealingly interesting. But he did produce at least some essays of this latter type.

The study/essay distinction provides here a handy tonal differentiation, one which also in this case becomes a fairly clear line of qualitative demarcation. Just as all of his fiction was made possible by it, Johnston's finest nonfiction comes from deep out of his own personal Georgia experience. "Historical" and "social" are not inappropriate adjectives for some of these productions, but the traditional meaning of *essay* which emphasizes the unique individual personality is the key to what makes these pieces distinctly valuable. By far Johnston's best pieces are those for which he utilized firsthand knowledge and those in which, consequently, his appealing and genial personality is an integral part of what is expressed. Johnston's four most noteworthy essays are evenly divisible according to the two qualities that his best fiction possesses: (1) value as social history, and (2) genuinely satisfying humor.

No essay comes closer to an inventory of the whole mental and spiritual warehouse of this man than his "Middle Georgia Rural Life" which appeared in *The Century* in March, 1892. Here the reminiscent, anecdotal Johnston is at his printed best on a topic upon which he often spoke formally and informally, a topic that vivified his own life no less completely than it informed his fiction. "A faithful sketcher of rural life in those times," writes this faithful sketcher of that antebellum society, "must have known to intimacy and loved and admired this people, and in boyhood must have been as green as the greenest in order to be put into sympathy indispensable to the just performance of his task."[31] This loving nonfictional recounting, says Professor L. Moody Simms, Jr., who was responsible for a 1974 reprinting of the essay, "represents one of the best contemporary accounts of rural life in nineteenth-century Middle Georgia and sheds light on the region's storytelling and literary background."[32] That the person rendering the account was a man of sensibility and a storyteller with a perennial twinkle in his eyes is pleasurably evident, and a valuable social document is rendered more valuable because of it. "Middle Georgia Rural Life" devotes much attention to the old-time legal fraternity of that region, among whose members Johnston had once been numbered.

"Early Educational Life in Middle Georgia," published in two parts as portions of the *Report of the [U.S.] Commissioner of Education* for the years 1894 - 95 and 1895 - 96, reports on another professional endeavor in which Johnston had even more, and more varied, experience. The first of these two "papers," as their author called them, begins with a general characterization of antebellum Middle Georgia society and proceeds to detailed descriptions of the classes, games, and special traditions of the Georgia old-field school. The second "paper" or part of the account picks up with "Vacation Time" and then considers the academies, a manual labor school, and the State University of Georgia.

Johnston would have been surprised and a little saddened had he lived to discover the opinion that his works of fiction "all together . . . do not equal in value the study of early educational life in Middle Georgia . . . prepared for the Commissioner of Education,"[33] but he himself had a good enough opinion of the piece to try to secure its publication in book form by a national commercial publisher. Although it is possible to see this long report as a "scholarly compilation,"[34] it is quite a different sort of scholarship or compilation from what Johnston executed with regard, say, to sixteenth-century England. "There are several occasions," he wrote Charles Dudley Warner about his educational "papers," "wherein a bit of humor, as it seemed to me, might be indulged, and I have tried to do so in apt places and times."[35] Surely one apt place and time was the beginning of the section on the old-time schoolmaster, probably the finest paragraph Johnston ever penned:

To an aged middle Georgian the old-field schoolmaster of his childhood, as he now recalls him, seems to have been somewhat of a myth, or at least a relic of a long past decedent race, never existing except in a few individuals unlike any others of human mold, appearing during periods in rural communities, bringing in a red-spotted bandanna handkerchief his household goods, and in his tall, whitish-furred, long-experienced hat a sheet of foolscap, on which was set down what he called his "school articles." A rather reticent man was he to begin with, generally serious, sometimes even sad looking, as if he had been a seeker of things occult and was not content with the results of his quest. Within some months, seldom completing the year, with the same bandanna and hat, noiseless as he had come, he went his way. Generally he was un- married, or, what was not so very far different, followed by a wife unique look- ing as himself, if possible some nearer a blank, who had never had the heart to increase the family any further. After his departure came on another, who might be larger and might be smaller, who might be fairer and might be browner, who might be more pronounced in manner and speech and might be less, but who had the distinctive marks that were worn by no other people under the sun.[36]

Two essays of Johnston's which appeared in *Lippincott's*, one in 1891 and the other in 1898, make their readers regret that Johnston did not write more light, informal personal pieces, pieces that docu- ment an individual's rather than a society's history. The first, "Reading Bores," considers with sympathetic whimsy the plight of the man whose best friend, so fond of reading aloud, is so blind to his inability to do it well. The essayist establishes immediately an attrac- tive tone and a bond with his reader:

City people are less sorely infected by these creatures than dwellers in small towns and villages, because in the former they are less often thrown into com- pelled, purposeless intercourse and have less leisure for boring and being bored. Rare as is the faculty of reading aloud well, it is curious that so many are fond of using what they possess. Unhappy is the man who has intimate friends in that class. Inflictions are to be borne during their joint lives. For of all of the infirmities to which mankind are subject, this same of reading ill and being fond of it is the last of whose existence they can be made aware. Have you (especially you of a village or small town) one such among your friends? Of course, you have, and I am sorry for you, and sympathize with you.[37]

The second of these familiar essays is even more appealing. In "Dogs and Railroad Conductors" Johnston discusses this incongruous pair of "races" whose constituents call forth his deepest fears and ap- prehensions. Being bitten by a dog in his youth, he says, "inspired ap- prehension of the canine race from which I long ago ceased to hope for relief in this life."[38] He is little comforted by dog owners who assure

him that their pets will not bite a gentleman. For if many persons cannot recognize a gentleman, he thinks, "what then can one expect of a
dog, who is not concerned to know about human characters, but is intent upon blood and meat?"[39] Railroad conductors must also be intent
upon something else, for their understanding in this regard is almost
as painfully obtuse. Gentle Southern gentility and inbred courtesy,
the essayist ineffectually recognizes, is precisely his problem in con-
tacts with these awesome personages:

Being forgetful and absent-minded, I need, or I seem to myself to need, to ask
a goodly number of questions when on a journey; yet, although I use the most
respectful and apologetic words, tones, and manners that I can invent, rising
from my seat, beginning with "Captain," and willing to begin with
"General" if preferred, and endeavor to show the personage that I regard him
as an unexhaustible and most gracious source of all needed information, how
do you suppose I feel, when, after all these offered amenities, a brief and in-
distinct if not a petulant answer is given in a low voice, and he rushes on?[40]

IV   *The Provincial Tourist*

In the fall of 1874 Richard Malcolm Johnston was viewing with increasing concern the decreasing enrollment at his Pen Lucy School.
However, he was, he reported, still "working with good heart," especially at night when "I am engaged with writing upon the subject of
my travels last year." The work in progress he planned as "a work of
about three hundred pages . . . partly sportive and fictitious, pur-
porting to be the work of Philemon Perch . . . ."[41] The travels
Johnston referred to were his travels in Europe; the "work," not published until 1885, was *Two Gray Tourists.*

The "gray" of the title may be taken to refer both to the age and the
past Confederate allegiance of the two old friends whose experiences
are recorded in these "Papers of Philemon Perch" "edited by Richard
Malcolm Johnston." Both sights and impressions have been set down,
says the editor's preface, but clearly it is the respective individual impressions and not descriptions of places that give this work its appeal.
The scenes of England, Scotland, Belgium, the Rhine region,
Switzerland, and France through which a "brief tour" is made are
simply structural, evocative, complementary necessities; as was usual
with Johnston, the true focus and real interest in *Two Gray Tourists* lie
in its Southern characters.

The main figures in this work, the two "gray tourists," are indeed
"characters"—Philemon Perch and Major Jim Rawls, native

Georgians and friends for over forty years. Philemon— as his creator and model and the ostensible editor of his travel "papers" describes him—is "a student, tall and slender, . . . sentimental, often absent-minded, and perhaps too fond of antiquarian research." Jim Rawls, on the other hand, is "a planter, stout, rather below middle height, . . . practical, entirely modern, energetic, and, on occasion, somewhat pugnacious." The two thus are complementary, and they are an entertaining pair. The amusing clash of their contrasting personalities is narrated in character and therefore at some length by the professorial Perch. One incident in England is very brief but is the epitome of both the tale and its telling:

> "To what base uses we descend," I remarked, as we looked toward where the ancient abbey once stood and saw only the gateway and another small part now used for a cowhouse.
> "A cow is a very useful animal, sir," said Jim.
> I looked at him reproachfully.[42]

The Macon *Telegraph* of October 26, 1885, reported that it found in *Two Gray Tourists* "a wealth of information pleasantly conveyed."[43] This assessment may be characteristic of contemporary reactions, for something in the book was popular and attractive enough to justify another edition in 1893. *Two Gray Tourists* is not, however, a production that can take front rank for substance, structure, or style among the numerous European travel accounts written by nineteenth-century Americans; it cannot compare, for example, with the very different works by Mark Twain, William Dean Howells, or Henry Adams which fall into this general category. Its extensive objective, historical tour-guide information may constitute "a wealth" for the uninitiated, but only the most patient reader can consistently experience pleasure in the ill-proportioned transmittal.

Pleasure from *Two Gray Tourists*—and positive amusement is to be had in a reading of this book—comes directly from the picaresque pair who achieve uniqueness in spite of their evident social representativeness and literary traditionalism. That the characters do this and that the book thus affords some enjoyment and enduring interest is because, as the *Telegram* noted, the genial personality of its author is everywhere manifested. For a person who is not interested in Johnston as a man, the book offers little; for one who is interested in Johnston's life and personality, it is intriguingly valuable.

Jimmy Ponder Voyles sees Philemon Perch and Jim Rawls as representing different aspects of Johnston as he reacts to Europe;

Johnston uses himself in order to use two characters to present different views of Europe and to dramatize the nineteenth-century controversy between progress and tradition, says Voyles.[44] Philemon Perch is an obvious reconstitution of Johnston as he most often saw himself and certainly as his contemporaries saw him. Johnston's lack of inventiveness and his general unwillingness or inability to indulge in introspection or serious analysis of any kind argue for a real-life model for Jim Rawls, and also argue that the model actually accompanied Johnston to Europe. Such a companion does not in fact seem to have existed. His old friend Edgar Dawson and he were in England together on Johnston's second trip abroad in 1874, but their projected trip to Scotland together was never realized. Dawson or Edgeworth Bird or another of his Georgia planter friends may have been his specific model, or Johnston may, atypically, have constructed a composite picture of this Southern type. But the character, however he came to life, seems to have been transported across the Atlantic by Johnston's imagination, a transposing and a creative act he was seldom capable of. The itinerary of *Two Gray Tourists* plainly follows that of his own European tour in the summer of 1873 when he chaperoned two American schoolboys. The "want of suitable companionship"[45] that he complained about on this trip appears, then, to have spurred an imaginative effort that had no Johnstonian precedent and that he scarcely matched later. His travel book, said Johnston, was "partly fictitious." His tales and sketches, also partly fictitious, represent in one sense less fiction, less imaginative re-creation than does *Two Gray Tourists*.

The tales and sketches are often cited for their value as social history, and the dialogue in *Two Gray Tourists* opens up social issues and social conditions in a way that is more direct but just as valuable. By means of these exchanges, Johnston comments at length, for example, on schoolkeeping and on postbellum social conditions in his native Georgia.

Revealing Philemon Perch's ideas and naiveté in this book, Johnston reveals his own. His letters from Europe tell essentially the same story as do Perch's "papers": the scholar who had written a literary history of England was movingly affected by the sights of things he had read about and even dreamed of for much of his life—but once in England he dreamed even more of returning home. Philemon Perch and Richard Malcolm Johnston, as their European sojourns prove, were incurably provincial. "Travel is the thing to knock the bottom out of a fellow's pride and his prejudices," argues Perch. But then he continues: "Yet all this don't keep me from being thankful, more so than before, if anything, for being born, and raised, and let live where I was."[46]

V   *The Lifelong* Life

No relationship outside his family meant more to Johnston than his thirty-year friendship with Alexander H. Stephens, the Vice President of the Confederacy and congressman and governor of Georgia. To Johnston, Stephens eventually became "my best friend,"[47] but long before then Johnston had decided that the older half-brother of Linton was worthy of a serious biography. The *Life of Alexander H. Stephens*, which was finally published in 1878 and issued in an enlarged version in 1883, was almost a lifelong work for the biographer. Had he not again secured the collaborative aid of William Hand Browne, the last twenty years of Johnston's life might well have been occupied as fully with the project as the middle twenty-five were.

Recording and explaining the facts of the life of his famous friend was a task to which Johnston had dedicated himself in 1856. On May 14 of that year he said in a letter to Stephens that "biography is the most interesting field in all literature to me" and revealed that the most interesting of all potential subjects within this field was, to him, Mr. Stephens.[48] Stephens's qualities of mind but especially of heart made him a man among men, Johnston believed, and he wanted the public to know these admirable qualities at a close second hand. He did not necessarily want to elucidate Stephens's public life or to justify his political stands, although these could not be ignored; rather, he repeatedly claimed, his purpose was to reveal the "inner nature" of this worthy and unselfish American who was, in his view, perhaps the noblest of the many noble sons of Middle Georgia. "Regarding it from every point of view," Johnston claimed on the last page of his own *Autobiography*, "the being of Alexander Stephens seemed to me the most unique of all with which I have been acquainted." Johnston recognized the vanity and the "native irascibility" of the man, but he saw wisdom and magnanimity here, too. "Of all persons whom I have ever known," the sensitive Johnston wrote, "his natural affections seemed to me the most passionate."[49]

Johnston's intimate acquaintance with Alexander Stephens he dated from the Know-Nothing campaign of 1855. Although they had known each other before, they came to be "on particularly friendly terms" then because of their common revulsion from Know-Nothingism and Johnston's admiration of Stephens's strong, principled action in opposing this movement. More particularly, Johnston sought the experienced Stephens's advice when he was being urged just after the campaign to accept a short-term judgeship; Stephens corroborated Johnston's views about not accepting the offer, and thus, recalled Johnston, the long friendship was begun. It was a relationship that "continued eventually with much intimacy" until the death of Stephens on March 4, 1883, not long after he had taken office as Governor of Georgia. Although he was listed officially as a pallbearer, Johnston apparently was unable to arrive in time for the funeral but instead wept alone in his study at Pen Lucy at that time and made a sad personal visit to Stephens's temporary grave a little later. In a eulogy delivered, by invitation, to the Georgia legislature upon his arrival in Atlanta, he spoke of Stephens's spiritual sufferings. "Twenty-five years of intimacy as entire and continuous as perhaps ever existed between two men," he said, "brought me into as full insight into these peculiar sufferings, and their causes, as is possible for one man to have into the interior life of another." [50]

Unfortunately, few Stephens-to-Johnston letters seem to have survived, but the many pieces of correspondence from Johnston to Stephens which exist paint the picture of a vital relationship. Letters between the two were surrogates for the visits and long conversations which both so enjoyed and whose infrequency they lamented. A mutual friend in New York admired above all the naturalness and truthfulness of the epistles that Stephens and Johnston sent to him, and these qualities in even purer form were to be found in their letters to each other. They assisted each other in living with the trials and triumphs of this life and in preparing for an existence in the next, a subject of no little discussion between them. As shown by his plaintive appeals for Johnston's visits during Stephens's last terms in Congress, it was not just a matter of hero worship on one hand and, on the other, the toleration or selfish promotion of such adoration. Genuine mutual dependence, love, and respect did cement their friendship. The respective salutations of the correspondence serve as comment on the relationship beyond simply the ten-year difference in age, however. Although to a third party Johnston would refer to his friend and biographical subject as "Alex," he never called Stephens anything but "Mr. Stephens" in his letters of over thirty years to the man; to Stephens, on the other hand, Professor or Colonel R. M. Johnston was "Dick."

Dick Johnston's part of the final biography was, as he saw it, the supremely important part having to do with Stephens's "home life," with the more private and personal aspects of the man's life. William Hand Browne's responsibility was for the political, for Stephens's public life, his roles on the wider stage of American history. For the facts in his area of responsibility Johnston relied upon Stephens's letters to him and upon their many conversations, some of which he tried to set down almost verbatim for later use. His mode of operation, as the final product shows too clearly, was generally scholarly. To cover the years before they became close friends Johnston obtained various other materials from Stephens, the most important being an early diary and the extensive correspondence between Alexander and Linton Stephens.

In both letters and conversations, his biographer early plied Stephens with questions. Not all inquiries could he get answered to his satisfaction, and so he came up with the scheme of initiating a correspondence between two fictitious characters, one "played" by Stephens and one whom he would portray. To "Jeems Giles," a subordinate in "Kernel" Johnston's household, came, then, replies from "Peter Finkle," whose patron was "Boss" Stephens. The Giles-Finkle correspondence flourished in 1863, but then lost its vigor of novelty. Johnston later attempted to draw Stephens out in a similar exchange between the imaginary kinsmen Colin and Arthur McNichol, but his efforts were to little avail this time.

The Giles-Finkle exchanges that were eventually so valuable for biographical purposes had their beginning in a prank—Johnston requesting criticism of some doggerel verse. Stephens was, in fact, one of the earliest and one of the best critics of Johnston's literary efforts, and although he read and approved the manuscript of the *Life* he was, unfortunately, not as critically astute and helpful with it as he had been with the manuscripts of the early stories. From his cultured collaborator William Hand Browne, Johnston received some fine critical and editorial assistance (including the reminder that it was a biography and not a panegyric he was writing), but Browne was a latecomer and knowingly a secondary agent in the enterprise.

Johnston entered earnestly upon the writing of the *Life* after his removal to Maryland, but the work went slowly and late in 1870 a concerned Stephens urged his friend to consider partnership with another, younger friend in Baltimore, J. Fairfax McLaughlin. This suggestion was not well received by Johnston, who, though, realizing that progress was slow, secured his "dear friend" Browne as a coworker in 1872. Johnston's letters to Stephens indicate that it was Browne who promoted an early publication of the work, not merely *before* Stephens's death (an action which, Johnston says, was not really his original intention) but, in fact, just as soon as it could be completed. A manuscript was ready by the summer of 1873, but there were difficulties with the Turnbulls, who had agreed to publish the book and who had even given an advance, and a misunderstanding about Stephens's disapproving parts of the work. Doing some rewriting, Johnston and Browne then sought a publisher outside Baltimore and, after getting several polite refusals, finally succeeded in reaching an agreement with Lippincott in Philadelphia.

Published in 1878, the *Life of Alexander H. Stephens* by Johnston and Browne received predominantly, though not exclusively, favorable reviews. The *New York Evening Sun* of September 17, 1878, for example, saw the work as in many respects a "model biography," and the Baltimore *Evening Bulletin* three days later called it "charming" and a "very artistic success." But such contemporary praise was excessive for a production that would later rightly be recognized as "formless"[51] and as possessing all "the usual defects of the authorized biography."[52]

In saying about the book "the style is just admirable, the narrative flows on with an easy grace and limpid simplicity that are full of beauty unadorned," the *Evening Bulletin* reviewer blindly pulled from his grab bag of pretty, meaningless phrases. The *Life* is plainly anything but this; what it is in reality is a draggy, unimaginative, patchwork affair that is mainly characterized by incoherence. In working with such voluminous materials and in attempting to let Stephens speak for himself, the authors came uninterestingly to do "little more than provide a running commentary on quoted letters and speeches."[53]

Although it was a labor of love and of much of a lifetime, Johnston's biography of Stephens can scarcely receive higher just evaluation than Edd Winfield Parks's finding it of "lasting value" because it is "an indispensable source-book."[54] Reviews of the *Life* may have been good, but its monetary returns and reputation-making ability were not high. He was both surprised and disgusted, J. W. Waddell wrote Stephens in 1880, that the needy and worthy Johnston had realized "so insignificantly" from the biography. While Waddell was, he commented, very pleased to hear that the Colonel was beginning to be paid quite liberally for magazine stories, this was all quite ironic now. For "surely he rested his hopes of future fame upon the Biography. What a humbug man, at his best is! and how delusive are his most confident expectations!"[55]

VI *For "those who have known me"*

His friend and admirer Bernard M. Steiner published a reminiscence of Johnston in *The Conservative Review* in February,

1899, a short piece which this periodical followed the next year with the posthumous publication of some autobiographical pieces and reminiscences by Johnston himself. Put together by the Neale Company and issued both in 1900 and 1901, these "notes" of "recollection" became the *Autobiography of Colonel Richard Malcolm Johnston.*

In his introduction Johnston relates the suggestion made to him by Henry M. Alden that he "write a book telling reminiscences of myself and others whom I had known." Unsure how interesting he could make these, Johnston did not immediately take his editor friend's advice. Later, though, when he had grown older and fonder of "looking back and admiring the past," he did so, hoping that the result would "be perused with interest by those who have known me, particularly those who have known me best."

For twentieth-century scholars who would like to know Johnston better, the *Autobiography* is a disappointment. Half of it is devoted not to Johnston himself, but to "men in prominent careers" and "of marked ability" in Middle Georgia—particularly Robert Toombs and Alexander H. Stephens. In the half that is more personal, Johnston ignores the very periods and activities for which illumination is especially desired: for example, the Civil War years; the difficult Maryland period of the late 1870s and early '80s; the personal literary activities and literary friendships of the late '80s and '90s. He does record some important biographical facts of the earlier part of his life and set forth some revealing opinions and details regarding the creation of his unique literature of Middle Georgia. Not surprisingly, the work as a whole, though, is lamentably superficial. Johnston had advertised only "reminiscences" and not a spiritual or intellectual history of any sort. But while they may be grateful for what it does provide, few persons will have for this autobiography the high regard that Johnston himself had for Goethe's.

In the *Autobiography* Johnston omits, as Edd Winfield Parks has recognized, "much that a stricter artistic integrity would have felt essential."[56] "His authobiography, like his stories," says Parks, "is unliterary."[57] Like both the stories and the rest of his large output of nonfiction, the *Autobiography* has no claim to art. Like the stories but unlike most of the nonfiction, it does have claim to at least some enduring value, however.

Most of Johnston's nonfiction is indeed "replaceable," but some of the essays, the Stephens biography, and his own fragmentary autobiography deserve to survive as "a contemporary source"[58] if nothing else. On these grounds, perhaps most of the local-color tales deserve survival. But like the best of the stories, the best of Johnston's nonfiction are the more personal pieces, and those, especially, that show the sportive rather than the serious side of the writer's personality.

CHAPTER 6

Coda

INTRODUCING sixty-six-year-old Richard Malcolm Johnston
at an authors' reading for international copyright in Washington in
1888, fifty-year-old Edward Eggleston spoke of his surprise at having
encountered Johnston's stories and then Johnston himself. In those
magazine stories by an unknown writer which began to appear a few
years before—stories "so full of quaint humor and individuality"—Eggleston had thought he'd seen, he said, "the hand of
a vigorous young man destined to make a name in our literature, and
to push us old fellows off the board, when once he should have
reached his maturity."[1] No doubt some members of the audience
were also surprised by "that promising young man," white-haired
and slightly stooped, whom Eggleston presented. If many of his contemporaries had no idea of the man's age, most Americans today have
no idea of the man. To be introduced to Johnston is for us not so much
a surprise as a revelation.

I   *The Place of Local Color*

Lawyer, educator, lecturer, author—R. M. Johnston, as he signed
most of his letters, falls generally and comfortably into that group of
later nineteenth-century American writers known as the local
colorists. The vogue of local-color writing in this country, mostly short
fiction in an age that Edgar Allan Poe accurately prophesied would be
a *magazine* age, is a phenomenon of American literary history which
dates from the late 1860s or early '70s through the mid to late 1890s.
Bret Harte's "The Luck of Roaring Camp" (1868) is usually said to
have initiated the movement, and, depending upon one's preference
for similarity or for difference, the appearance of Sarah Orne Jewett's
The Country of the Pointed Firs (1896) or Charles Major's *When
Knighthood Was in Flower* (1898) may be regarded as signaling its
end.[2]

128

Not without earlier roots, of course, local-color writing flowered after the blood bath of the Civil War. The desire for reconciliation that created an intense interest in "other" sections of the nation is one often-cited reason, as is, on the other hand, an increased concern about one's own section of the country, especially preserving its old ways and unique traditions in the face of an urbanizing, standardizing, frighteningly different postbellum society.

The war gave strong new motives to both literary Romanticism and Realism. While the general disillusionment of war served to make writers and readers disdainful of romantic, idealistic treatments of life, experiencing the horrible realities of armed conflict and, in the South, of ignominious defeat also pushed them, perhaps more insistently, toward refuge in a nostalgic ideality.

Compelling conflicting influences directly related to literary nationalism were also produced. The United States, having emerged from this epic struggle, was at last confirmed as a nation. The Great Democratic Experiment had finally proven itself to the rest of the world, and an earlier but temporarily suspended Romantic impulse now called for a distinctive literature commensurate with the supposed millennial nation. Effecting this Romantic notion shifted the nation's writers toward Realism, however. For if America was historically justified and worthy now, was not recent, actual American life precisely and necessarily what its great national literature should treat?

Whatever the many complex reasons, the final product was assuredly different. "With the conclusion of the war between North and South, American fiction enters upon a new era," reported *The Edinburgh Review* in 1891; "the date forms a watershed, a 'Great Divide.' "[3] Whereas, continued this reviewer, "before 1861 writers of American fiction were either imitators or [were] not distinctively national," later novels and short stories emerging from the United States are distinctively American, the reason being that American fiction between 1865 and 1891 "mainly devoted itself to the task of delineating contemporary life with fulness of detail and fidelity to truth."[4]

From the present vantage point of almost a century Herbert F. Smith claims that, with the rise of Realism as its opening esthetic, "the second American renaissance, comparable at all points to the first, which F. O. Matthiessen described, can be dated at approximately 1880 - 1885."[5] The local colorists of this time may be seen merely as forming "a kind of backdrop for the great works on center stage,"[6] but they may also legitimately be regarded as having realized the circumstances and vivified the esthetic that made possible the masterpieces of Mark Twain, William Dean Howells, and Henry James.

In distinguishing between two practicing schools of American fiction, the writer on American literature in the 1891 *Edinburgh Review* recognized rather casually what Americans were proclaiming much more pointedly: by necessity, a distinctive American literature would have to be and was being achieved by sections; that the great diversity of American civilization would allow it no other way. "Local life" must be the basis of any live literature, wrote Thomas Wentworth Higginson in 1892, and he noted with pleasure that "all the varied elements of our society are being rapidly sought out and exhibited": "In a comparatively new country, especially, the first essential of a permanent literature—more essential at first than great works of history, philosophy, or poetry—is a wide multiplicity of works of really admirable local fiction. This is precisely what we have now accomplished."[7] To anyone who had seen this wide multiplicity, Nathaniel Hawthorne's observation in the late 1850s would have seemed prophetic. America, Hawthorne had said, has "no limits and no oneness; and when you try to make it a matter of the heart, everything falls away except one's native State."[8]

But even individual states, it turned out, did not suffice. As Maurice Thompson observed, American writers of the late nineteenth century were working in "literary half-acres."[9] And there were many acres of such real estate, many extremely fertile little garden plots. Probably the writers most prominently and immediately associated with the local-color movement are: from the Northeast—Sarah Orne Jewett, Mary E. Wilkins Freeman, and Rose Terry Cooke; from the West—Bret Harte; from the Midwest—Hamlin Garland; and, from the South—George Washington Cable, Joel Chandler Harris, Thomas Nelson Page, and Mary Noailles Murfree. But in New England there were also Harriet Beecher Stowe, Alice Brown, and Rowland E. Robinson; in the West, Joaquin Miller and Mary Hallock Foote; in the Midwest, Edward Eggleston, Mary Hartwell Catherwood, Maurice Thompson, and Constance Fenimore Woolson; in the old Middle States, Margaret Deland and Philander Deming; in the South, Richard Malcolm Johnston, Sherwood Bonner, Kate Chopin, and Grace King. The lists could go on and on—Gertrude Atherton, Alfred Henry Lewis, Thomas A. Janvier, Sarah Pratt Green, Will Allen Dromgoole, James Weber Linn, Charles F. Lummis, Abraham Cahan, Philip Verrill Mighels, Esther B. Carpenter, John Habberton. From the South the roster seems truly interminable:

Virginia Frazer Boyle, Francis Hopkinson Smith, James Lane Allen, John Fox, Jr., Will N. Harben, Ruth McEnery Stuart, Harry Stillwell Edwards, Matt Crim, Charles W. Chesnutt, Alice French, Sarah Barnwell Elliott, Mollie E. Moore Davis, Constance Cary Harrison. . . . The names are legion, and the number of works, of course, even more so.

Although the role and the value of local-color fiction in American literary history have been noted above, doubts about the intrinsic literary merit of the work of the local colorists existed at the height of the movement, and with the passage of time these doubts have been vindicated. In his "Literary Half-Acres" Maurice Thompson had deplored such literary "specialism" as he perceived the writers of local-color fiction to be engaged in. "It goes without saying," he nevertheless said, "that vast and varied crops cannot be grown on a quarter-acre farm. . . . The flowers and fruits are highly colored and are sometimes of a novel fragrance; but the powerful perfume of original nature and the flavor of universal human appeal are not present."[10] An autopsy of the local-color phenomenon ("the cult of local color") in *The Nation* in 1919 disclosed the "triviality of observation" that followed inevitably from the "surface singularities" of the various locales; from the first, it was claimed, the emphasis was on *local* rather than on *color*.[11] Fifty-two years later a glossary for students of English emphasized the distinction between regional literature on the one hand and local-color literature on the other. "Both," it said, "are concerned with an accurate depiction of the manners, morals, dialects, and scenery of a particular geographical area." *But* "generally, 'local color' is a mildly pejorative term, describing works that, however pleasant, have little value other than the portrayal of life in a given area. . . ."[12] Historically, says Claud B. Green, to apply the term to writers "means that these writers did their best work in the period from 1870 to 1900 and that their best work has not been considered good enough to lift them out of the category of the local-color school."[13] "At its best," concludes Octave Thanet's biographer, local color "was skillful and perceptive, and in the case of such an expert as Mary Wilkins Freeman or Sarah Orne Jewett or Alice French it was sometimes even moving; but it was never profound."[14]

II *The Place of Richard Malcolm Johnston*

Profundity, perceptiveness, evocativeness, and expertise are not terms that dash to mind to characterize the writings of Richard

Malcolm Johnston. At best, only a few of the incidents and some few more of his characters even if all of his little geographical "half-acre" achieve a life of their own. Johnston's writing, however, has an historical importance and a natural interest matched by only a handful of the most gifted and expert of the local colorists. And, unusual and significant in such "historical value" cases, he is as noteworthy for his uniquenesses as for his representativeness.

For the literary or cultural or intellectual historian, the representative or the epitomic is itself significant, of course. Johnston is in many ways a fine generic example of the local colorist, a revealing representative of this literary movement which has also been characterized by such terms as "flood" and "craze" and "passion." A perusal of his fiction will illustrate clearly the critical commonplaces regarding local-color stories—the preoccupation with, and faithful, detailed depiction of, a limited geographical area; the use of dialect; the idealization of the past; the use of sentiment and avoidance of the unpleasant; the frequent happy ending; the concentration of the peculiarities of a region and the individualities of its people; the resultant emphasis on "picturesque oddities"; the concern for the poor or the "common folk."[15]

From another but contiguous perspective Johnston's work may also be fruitfully studied for the light that it sheds on the reading tastes of the American public and the, in part at least, consequent predilections and prejudices of literary editors of his time. In his later, nationally known work, although it was in entire accord with his own predilections, Johnston was clearly and successfully supplying the American public with the kind of reading material it liked.

A close look at Johnston's professional literary career corroborates the labeling of the latter half of the nineteenth century as "the age of the magazine" and serves to support claims about the influence of this form of mass-circulation publication upon the development of American literature. The negotiations and careful wranglings as well as the sincere mutual delight of the editor-contributor relationship are open to revealing view with Johnston. Also, Johnston, like so many other writers of his time, took to the reading platform and the lecture tour. And, like many of them, he was a member of the organization of American authors actively working—successfully this time—for international copyright legislation.

Like some other of the local colorists, R. M. Johnston achieved national prominence through his writings. Highly regarded by both the public and the profession—though probably more by the latter if one regard or the other were higher—he drew encomia from such friends and acquaintances as William Dean Howells, Samuel L. Clemens, Charles Dudley Warner, and Edmund Clarence Stedman. He was deliberately and urgently included in the November 28 - 29, 1887, American Copyright League readings at Chickering Hall in New York, which more than one knowledgeable observer regarded as the most notable and remarkable gathering of literary men that America had ever witnessed.[16] Another invitation he accepted was to the White House. Johnston, *The Baltimore Sun* recorded without exaggeration at the time of his death, held a distinguished place among American men of letters, his literary work having achieved high rank in both popular and critical appreciation.[17] The man was especially highly appreciated personally, and in one way even this was representative. For, particularly to many Northern Americans, "Colonel" Johnston—tall, white-haired, exceedingly genial, markedly courteous, lover of mint juleps, and purveyor of a fetching drawl—was the supreme incarnation of the mythical old Southern gentleman. There is even reason to believe, on the good authority of Harry Stillwell Edwards, that Johnston was the model for F. Hopkinson Smith's epitomic Southern gentleman "afta de wah," the irrepressible and irresistible Colonel Carter of Cartersville.

In an exclusively Southern context, Johnston, of course, looms larger and more important, and his claims or attractions are, increasingly, more unique than representative. Johnston's little literary territory was Middle Georgia, and both the territory and the time he occupied it literarily are significant. The decline of his critical reputation, as Fred Lewis Pattee points out, "has been as sudden as his rise, and yet in one respect he is a notable figure in the history of the short-story form: *Dukesborough Tales* in its various editions shows the evolution of the American *genre* sketch from the primitive Longstreet model, coarse and brutal . . . through . . . softening and artistic influence . . . to . . . sketches carefully subdued and finished."[18] Although Pattee's implications are national, his context and foundations are firmly and necessarily Southern. Whenever, in fact, Johnston's critical reputation has not declined to the point of ignorance, his major literary significance is seen in his pivotal, transitional position between the Old Southwest humorists and the later, especially the Southern, local colorists, many of whom also wrote with a fine sense of the comic. Johnston, says Walter Blair in his study of American humor, is "one author who very clearly shows a relationship between the older humor and the newer local color writing"; he is, according to Wade Hall, a scholar of Southern humor, "the writer who best illustrates the changing humor of the Civil War period." Hall's term for Johnston is "transitionist," while "a link" and "the link" are the characterizing choices of Clarence Gohdes and Fred Lewis Pattee. Johnston's writings, says Carlos Baker in the *Literary History of the United States*, are plainly in the tradition of A. B. Longstreet, J. J. Hooper, and W. T. Thompson, and in his works one sees "a combination of the rugged virtues of the old with a new and pervasive sympathy and a restrained use of sentiment."[19]

Johnston occupies, then, a unique and distinctive place in Southern and, not just incidentally, in Georgia's literary history. Because he had been writing and publishing in obscurity so much earlier, his popularity as a result of the local-color craze makes him probably the best single illuminator of the altered conditions and opportunities for postbellum writers from the American South. Seen as a significant transition figure, Johnston can thus also be viewed as the first of a distinctive new generation of Southern writers. To George Washington Cable should probably go first honors for opening up the field of Southern literature to a national audience, but perhaps because Cable's materials were so exotic, so unrepresentative of the larger, mostly rural South, the distinction quite often goes to Johnston.

Some question may be made of the 1880s constituting a renaissance for American literature, but there can be no doubt about its being a Southern literary renaissance. Following the West and the Northeast in regional turns, the South, as Robert Underwood Johnson said, "was in the literary saddle in those days."[20] Richard Malcolm Johnston "is justly recognized," wrote Edmund Clarence Stedman in 1898, "as the founder of a school of fiction and the dean of Southern men of letters."[21] Playing too much the academic literary historian, one can point to Johnston's stories in the 1850s and '60s and reckon him "with Harte as a pioneer" in the whole local-color movement.[22] More accurately and honestly it can be said simply that "Johnston was to the Southern movement what Eggleston was to the Western."[23]

No one who has read much of Richard Malcolm Johnston's fiction can doubt that "the center and soul of his art was the Georgia environment."[24] More specifically, it was the environment of Middle Georgia, and more specifically than that, it was Hancock County, Georgia. "The wit and humor of Georgia stand by themselves," claimed Joel Chandler Harris; "they have no counterpart in any other section of the country."[25] And Harris was himself more specific. "If," he wrote on another occasion, "you will take a map of Georgia, pick out Putnam County, and then put your finger on the counties sur-rounding it—Morgan, Greene, Hancock, Baldwin, Jones, and Jasper—you will have under your thumb the seat of Southern humor."[26] Harris's opinion is, of course, a partisan, participatory one, but it is both true and truly extraordinary how many writers who at-tained national prominence came from this comparatively small geographical area. What might be called the Georgia literary succes-sion of the nineteenth century offers a fascinating possibility for en-vironmental impact study. The diadem, as it were, passed from the founder of the line Augustus Baldwin Longstreet (1790 - 1870) to William Tappan Thompson (1812 - 1882) to Charles Henry Smith ["Bill Arp"] (1826 - 1903) to Richard Malcolm Johnston (1822 - 1898) to Joel Chandler Harris (1848 - 1908) to Harry Stillwell Edwards (1855 - 1938).

Various collective and individual literary claims may be made for this "line," but these men have especially important claims as social historians, each of his own little temporal and geographic territory. As has been said specifically of Johnston, whose forte was the school and educational life, whatever their virtues or their defects, these writers will live "because of their fidelity to a vanished area of American life."[27] In the semirealistic writings of the Southern humorists, as Cle-ment Eaton notes, there runs a rich vein of social history: these writers "present through their imagination and firsthand knowledge of the plain people a kind of truth that eludes the researcher in documents."[28]

Johnston's own biographical documents exist today because of his literary reputation, but one can discover and make claims for the in-herent importance, interest, and instructiveness of the life of this man who, though long hopeful, was for so long only incidentally a man of letters. And here, in the unique turns and twists of an individual human life, is absolute distinctiveness. If, in some ways, Johnston's fiction may be regarded as both unique and representative, the weight falls upon the latter. If, similarly, his literary career may be seen as both unique and representative, the weight here is clearly with the unique. Johnston was, as Jay B. Hubbell points out, the amateur who finally—and rather desperately and fortuitously—turned professional.[29] Embarking upon a professional writing career at the age of fifty-seven and bursting into the national limelight at age sixty-one, he was, however, so prolific in consequent production that the case seemed to E. C. Stedman seriously "to weaken the theory that a writer's creative force lessens year by year in the afternoon of life."[30]

Johnston's years as a rural circuit lawyer and as a teacher bear definite fruit in his literary productions, but, a reforming and influential educator, he has some right to unalloyed distinction in this field. A leader in the "new" private academy movement of Georgia, he also was in the vanguard of the establishment of "English" as an academic subject for college study. He was much else as well: a biographical Boswell to his own Johnson—Alexander H. Stephens, the Vice President of the Confederacy; a serious scholar who turned down a judgeship and a college presidency to become a professor; a reformed hothead and unreformed slave owner who opposed secession but who stuck by his native state during the war; the son of a Baptist preacher and the very first graduate of Mercer University who was converted, with consequences good and ill, to Roman Catholicism; a man who delighted in his colonelcy but who quite deliberately was never a soldier; a gentleman, penurious but proud, who actively sought and faithfully filled a lowly bureaucratic clerkship. Such a man was the genial and ingenuous Georgian who once was known and, mostly, not known to the world as "Philemon Perch."

If they can only meet him, Carl Holliday predicted, "there will be a smile for him in generations to come."[31] There may even be a tear as well.

III   *"Literature and Life"*

R. M. Johnston, "that promising young man" whom Edward Eggleston introduced to a distinguished capital city audience in 1888, would eventually see in print eighty-three short stories or tales, all but four of them collected in a total of ten different books; four novels or novellettes in book form; five assorted books of nonfiction; fifty-three personal, social, historical, or literary essays and speeches, twenty of which were collected in two autograph volumes; seven separately printed public addresses; and one poem. His finest pieces lie among the short fiction and the reminiscent essays, but none even here can make strong claim to art. While in his own time he was praised for the intrinsic merit of his works as well as for his general literary activity, today his literary activity is what has secured his salvation from oblivion. The deliverance should not, however, be unwelcome.

"I have never been able," William Dean Howells once wrote, "to see much difference between what seemed to me Literature and what seemed to me Life. . . . Unless the thing seen reveals to me an intrinsic poetry and puts on phrases that clothe it pleasingly to the imagination, I do not much care for it; but if it will do this, I do not mind how poor or common or squalid it shows at first glance: it challenges my curiosity and keeps my sympathy."[32] At least some of the literature that Richard Malcolm Johnston produced still has life in it, and certainly the life of this old-time Georgian is literary in several senses.

Johnston became a genuine and respected member of the American literary community of the late nineteenth century.[33] His local-color stories were his entree, and his age, personality, and circumstances his ultimate retainer. To Edmund Clarence Stedman he was "the dean of Southern men of letters"; to Bernard Steiner, "The Nestor of Southern Literary Men"; to James Whitcomb Riley, "the Vicar of Wakefield of American Literature." To William Dean Howells he was simply "my old friend and honored brother-in-letters."[34] To the discerning editor of *The Dial* in 1898, Johnston could be viewed as "without a rival" in the literary exhibition of "manners in Georgia half a century ago." But more discriminatingly and conclusively, as *The Dial* went on to say, the books the man wrote "are at the same time [only] *acceptable* works of fiction . . . [while] *important* historical documents."[35]

From several intermediary perspectives and in a final proper one, Johnston's major importance must be reckoned as historical. The career of Thomas Chatterton he considered the most eccentric among all those of British writers, and the historian of American literature can come close to saying the same of Johnston among writers of the United States. A man who "set more value upon the scholarly than the creative because he had no doubt about the worthiness of doing that kind"[36] of writing, he suddenly gained national reputation on the basis of the creative when he was over sixty years of age. He had earlier, it must be recognized, earnestly sought wider publication for his fiction, but he probably spoke the truth when he said that the favor finally given it was more than he expected "and more, as I sincerely feel, than I deserve."[37] Swept into a belated popularity by the great tide of Local Color, his work was rediscovered, and he moved quickly and diligently to transform the rough early pieces into more refined, genteel patterns. An old man by then, he might naturally have shifted emphasis away from "the humorous effect of a particular tale" and have become much "more intent on preserving a record of something fast disappearing from the earth than in catching something which seemed likely to stay alive."[38] Without the coincidence of peculiar national literary conditions and a personal condition of

penuriousness, this question would not now be open, however. And
American literary history would be without a superb single illustrator
of the transition from humorists of the Old Southwest to the
acclaimed Southern local colorists of the late nineteenth and early
twentieth centuries.

Johnston's seventy-six year lifetime spanned nearly unbelievable
changes in American, and especially Southern American, life and
culture. Even before 1875 he was wondering, he said, whether he was
still on the same planet where as a boy he had played along the waters
of Powel's Creek in Hancock County, Georgia.[39] Responding to E. C.
Stedman's comment about the seemingly perennial greenness of his
heart, Johnston revealed the lifeblood of all of his literary productions
when he spoke of his childhood recollections. "My memory for thirty
years and more," he wrote, "has been dwelling mainly on that happy
period. When I think about getting up one and another little story, my
heart takes my mind back there. I never could see that I could make
any thing of material taken from any where else."[40]

Johnston's frequently expressed purpose of illustrating characters
and incidents of Middle Georgia life in his stories and of making them
"in entire harmony with the real"[41] looks toward the undeniable
value of his works for the social historian. His added phrase of "drawn
from memory" or "as I recall" is, however, a clear warning to the
historian, who knows how fondly and distortingly human beings look
back to the good old times that are no more. Perhaps nowhere is
Johnston's own recognition of this so clear as in a speech he made in
Atlanta in 1857. Ironically, he urged his auditors to remain in Georgia,
but prophetically he also advised, "Look into the past!" "How
precious are its recollections!" he said. "The joys and the griefs, the
smiles and the tears, what we have enjoyed alike with what we have
suffered, on the wings of memory they come to us, and strange and
unaccountable is the fond sadness, which makes us the wiser, and
sometimes, we think, the better and the happier!"[42]

The reservations of the social historian about Johnston's tales are
founded no differently from those of the literary critic. For works of
the nostalgic and "maximally affirmative"[43] Johnston, the serious
critic must have some serious reservations. The "fond sadness" which
came "on the wings of memory" to inform his local-color stories too
often resulted in idealization and melodrama, too often imposed itself
with shrill notes of didacticism. Johnston no doubt, as he claimed, did
love the people of Middle Georgia whom he sought to illustrate, but
from the distance of revolutionary decades, he

loved too fondly. He believed a "cordial human sympathy . . . is at the bottom of all humor that is genuine," but sweet as even this humor was, pathos was sweeter.[44] Both the facts of that provincial Georgia life as he remembered it and the facts of a broader morality as he saw it Johnston intended his works of fiction to convey. "Essentially," said Edd Winfield Parks, "Johnston represents the author as teacher, not the author as artist." As genuine as some of the humor may be and as faithful as are some representations of some aspects of the society, too many of his working literary principles deny art and "rob . . . much of his work of any ultimate reality."[45]

Although W. A. Webb saw Johnston's limitations as "readily apparent," and believed that it would require no very astute critic to note immediately "that his work as a whole is marked by a narrowness of range and paucity of incident,"[46] numerous contemporary critics— including William Dean Howells, Charles Dudley Warner, H. M. Alden, R. W. Gilder, and Edmund Clarence Stedman—noted much that was praiseworthy both in Johnston's individual works and in his work as a whole. This praise is often impressively high, but seldom does another impression fail to be made: that however superb what appears in print, the experiencing of Richard Malcolm Johnston in person would immeasurably enhance or else completely eclipse the value of reading his works. Bernard M. Steiner best brings into focus what is implicit in contemporary review after contemporary review. "I pity those," wrote Steiner, "who have never seen Colonel Johnston and yet take up any of his writings. It may be that a new generation can pass the stories by as we pass by Longstreet's 'Georgia Scenes,' but that will only be because the person of the Colonel will be unknown to it."[47]

Perhaps a later generation will return to Johnston's works of fiction as a new generation did in fact go back appreciatively to *Georgia Scenes*. At this point, however, as in 1938, "it would be foolish to attempt to revive them."[48] Edd Winfield Parks's sympathetic but realistic judgment of Johnston forty years after his death can scarcely be equaled for judiciousness. For any study of the life and works of this "intelligently simple"[49] man who knew the classics of world literature only a little less intimately than he knew the plain folks of rural Georgia, it is a fitting epilogue:

His novels and the majority of his stories have some value as a part of our social and critical history: they reveal the manner in which local colorists were the heritors of the earlier humorists, and they describe one part of a life well worth living. They serve as texts, and there is irony in the fact that it is this portion of his work which has the greatest historical and scholarly value. A few stories—certainly less than a dozen—may continue in their own right, barely discernible above a choppy surface which even now threatens to submerge them. They deserve to remain. If they are tales and sketches rather than stories, if they have the natural growth of expanded oral incidents with small aid from art, if they give one part of life instead of a whole, these stories re-create within their slight translated world a few humorous, pathetic, simple, vital characters, a little town in middle Georgia, and a culture which grew out of a way of living.[50]

Notes and References

Chapter One

1. In the preface to his University of Georgia dissertation "Richard Malcolm Johnston: A Biographical and Critical Study" (1971) Jimmy Ponder Voyles laments the "dearth of objective information" about Johnston and accurately points out the "lack of present adequate biographical treatments" of the man. Voyles, of course, had remedial intentions, and this dissertation, while obviously not entirely biographical, is to date the single most valuable and trustworthy secondary source of information about Johnston's life. More detailed and accessible, and very informative though intentionally limited in scope, are Edd Winfield Parks's "Professor Richard Malcolm Johnston" in the March, 1941, number of *The Georgia Historical Quarterly* and Francis Taylor Long's three-part treatment of Johnston's Baltimore years in the *Maryland Historical Magazine* (numbers in 1939, 1940, and 1941). A number of other secondary sources make valuable specific biographical contribution, but they lack either the depth or reliability, or both, of these three studies. A "dearth" or a "lack" may indeed be said to exist, and while this chapter cannot be exhaustive in its treatment, it does aim toward some conclusiveness. Johnston's *Autobiography* is, of course, an essential source of biographical information, but it is as notable for what it distorts, contradicts, or ignores as for what it includes. Because statements from the *Autobiography* are, it seems to me, easily retrievable, I do not in this chapter note specific page numbers for quotations from this source. Basic to a more objective depiction of Johnston's life, and utilized here more inclusively than in any previous study, are primary and near-primary materials relating to Johnston—his letters especially but also the letters of his family, various manuscripts, and contemporary newspaper clippings. These materials exist in surprisingly large numbers and in a surprising number of collections. The largest and most important are the Richard Malcolm Johnston Collection at the Enoch Pratt Free Library in Baltimore, the Alexander H. Stephens Papers in the Library of Congress, and the Johnston Collection (including the invaluable research notes of F.T. Long) at the Georgia Historical Society in Savannah. Somewhat smaller but still significant Johnston holdings are in the manuscript collections at Duke University, Emory University, Trinity College, Columbia University, and Indiana University.

2. B.D. Ragsdale, *Story of Georgia Baptists* (Atlanta, 1932), I, 239.

3. *The Triennial Register of Mercer University*, 1897 - 98, pp. 5 - 6.

4. Lessie Brannen Brinson, "A Study of the Life and Works of Richard Malcolm Johnston," Diss. George Peabody 1937, p. 25.

5. *The Triennial Register of Mercer University,* 1897 - 98, p. 6. While these three men are legitimately considered as the first graduating class of Mercer, P.S. Whitman (a Brown graduate) was awarded an honorary degree with this group.

6. Copy of July 29, 1891, letter to Mrs. W.G. Charlton (Mary Walton Johnston), in the Johnston Collection, Georgia Historical Society.

7. These letters are in the Johnston Collection, Georgia Historical Society.

8. Johnston to Alexander H. Stephens, November 26, 1869 (Library of Congress), and to E.C. Stedman, December 26, 1894 (Butler Library, Columbia University). Both are cited in the Voyles dissertation, pp. 19 and 77 respectively, although the December 3 date given the Stedman letter there and by Columbia is disproved by the contents of the letter itself.

9. Johnston formally dedicated his *Lectures on Literature: English, French and Spanish* (1897) to his wife, whom he now had lost to death. The penned inscription appears in his hand over the date of July 10, 1897, in the copy of the book which was in his personal library and which is now in the Maryland Collection at the Enoch Pratt Free Library in Baltimore.

10. Mary Ann Mansfield to her father, Giles Mansfield, February 23, 1845, and April 29, 1845, in the Johnston Collection, Georgia Historical Society.

11. See James D. Waddell, *Biographical Sketch of Linton Stephens* (Atlanta, 1877). In addition to some Stephens-Johnston correspondences, Waddell reproduces (pp. 177 - 188) the long letter that Johnston wrote in 1873 in response to Waddell's request for reminiscences of Linton Stephens.

12. Another of these friendships, and one of even longer duration, was that between Johnston and Alexander Stephens. This relationship is considered at some length in the section of Chapter 5 that deals with Johnston's and William Hand Browne's *Life of Alexander H. Stephens.*

13. Alexander H. Stephens Papers, Library of Congress. This and many other passages from the Johnston letters included here are quoted by Voyles, whose dissertation is the first and a significant utilization of this important source of biographical information.

14. Typed copy in the William Gilmore Simms papers in Duke University Library.

15. Joel Chandler Harris, *Stories of Georgia* (New York, 1896), p. 241.

16. William Henry Sparks, *The Memories of Fifty Years,* 3rd ed. (Philadelphia, 1872), p. 482.

17. Richard Malcolm Johnston, "Middle Georgia Rural Life," *Century,* 43 (March 1892), 740.

18. Waddell, p. 182.

19. For a detailed study of Georgia politics from 1845 to 1861, see Horace Montgomery, *Cracker Parties* (Baton Rouge, Louisiana, 1950).

20. I.W. Avery, *The History of the State of Georgia, from 1850 to 1881.* (New York, 1881), p. 42.

21. Clipping in the Johnston Collection, Georgia Historical Society.

22. Parks's article, "Professor Richard Malcolm Johnston," *Georgia Historical Quarterly*, 25 (March 1941), 1 - 15, and Johnston's letters to Alexander and Linton Stephens, in the Alexander H. Stephens Papers, Library of Congress, are the best sources of information for this period of Johnston's life, and this section on the University of Georgia draws heavily upon them. Parks has carefully reviewed minutes of the trustees' meetings and other official documents in the archives of the University.

23. Bernard Suttler, "Richard Malcolm Johnston," in *Men of Mark in Georgia*, ed. William J. Northen (1911; rpt. Spartenburg, S.C., 1974), p. 470.

24. "My Schools," *Lippincott's*, 54 (November 1894), 706.

25. Arthur N. Applebee, *Tradition and Reform in the Teaching of English: A History* (Urbana, Illinois, 1974), p. 10.

26. See especially Chapter X, "Revolt and Reorganization," of E. Merton Coulter's *College Life in the Old South*, 2nd ed. (Athens, Georgia, 1951).

27. April 17, 1861, letter to Alexander H. Stephens, A.H. Stephens Papers, Library of Congress. Unless otherwise noted, all references to Johnston-A.H. Stephens correspondence are to items in this collection.

28. March 11, 1861, letter to Linton Stephens in the Alexander H. Stephens Papers, Library of Congress.

29. Again the letters from Johnston in the Alexander H. Stephens Papers are most valuable, but other important information specifically about this period may be found in the Johnston Collection at the Georgia Historical Society and in Johnston's own article "My Schools" in the November, 1894, *Lippincott's*.

30. Letter of July 16, 1860, in the Herschel V. Johnson Papers, Duke University Library.

31. Voyles, p. 41.

32. Regina Armstrong, "Richard Malcolm Johnston, Gentleman and Man of Letters," *Catholic World*, 68 (November 1898), 270.

33. As noted earlier, the Voyles dissertation and Francis T. Long's "The Life of Richard Malcolm Johnston in Maryland, 1867 - 1898" in the *Maryland Historical Magazine* 34 (December 1939), 305 - 324; 35 (September 1940), 270 - 286; 36 (March 1941), 54 - 69 are the best secondary sources for information about Johnston's life in Maryland. General indebtedness to these, to the *Autobiography*, and to the previously recognized primary sources continues, specific reference and citation being given when appropriate.

34. In the Sallie Donelson Hubert Papers, Duke University Library.

35. Johnston to Matthew Hubert, August 6, 1880, in the Sallie Donelson Hubert Papers, Duke University Library.

36. Lanier to Johnston, July 5, 1881, in the Richard Malcolm Johnston Collection, Enoch Pratt Free Library, Baltimore, Maryland.

37. Johnston to E.C. Stedman, September 14, 1888, in the Butler Library, Columbia University. Ownership by the Columbia University Libraries of

the original manuscripts in their Edmund C. Stedman Collection is hereby acknowledged.

38. Johnston to Stedman, August 12, 1894, and August 27, 1894, Butler Library, Columbia University.

39. Johnston to Charles Dudley Warner, February 21, 1896, in the Watkinson Library at Trinity College, Hartford, Connecticut.

40. Johnston to Stedman, July 4, 1889, Butler Library, Columbia University.

41. R.M. Johnston to Effie Johnston, May 22, 1897, in the Johnston Collection, Georgia Historical Society.

42. G. W. Cable to Miss Johnston, September 24, 1898, in the Richard Malcolm Johnston Collection, Enoch Pratt Free Library, Baltimore, Maryland.

Chapter Two

1. There is evidence, primarily in letters from Johnston to A.H. Stephens, that this project was much more Johnston's own idea and personal undertaking than is here implied. The designation "private printing" may not, in fact, be inaccurate.

2. *Dukesborough Tales* (New York, 1892), p. 2. Unless otherwise noted, quotations from the respective Dukesborough tales are taken from the last edition in which the tale appears. Page numbers for extended quotations in this chapter will hereafter be given in parentheses after the quotation.

3. Ima Honaker Herron, *The Small Town in American Literature* (1939; rpt. New York, 1959), p. 328.

4. William A. Webb, "Richard Malcolm Johnston," *Southern Writers: Biographical and Critical Studies*, II (1903; rpt. New York, 1970), p. 69.

5. In some ways Johnston's Dukesborough collections thus look forward to such works as Sherwood Anderson's *Winesburg, Ohio* (1919) and Ernest Hemingway's Nick Adams stories in *In Our Time* (1925). Johnston's use of grotesque characters, noted more specifically in the next chapter, also anticipates Anderson as well as such twentieth-century Southern writers as Flannery O'Connor, Carson McCullers, Eudora Welty, and William Faulkner, who have made the grotesque a notable aspect of Southern fiction.

6. Clara Ruth Coleman Wood, "The Fiction of Richard Malcolm Johnston," Diss. University of North Carolina, Chapel Hill, 1973, p. 214.

7. Because the 1892 version (p. 48) omits mention of the iron sole shoes, I have here used the 1871 edition of *Dukesborough Tales*.

8. William Howard, "Three Nineteenth-Century Georgia Humorists," Thesis Auburn University 1950, p. 163.

9. Whether or not Johnston's story is the source for such an episode in *The Adventures of Huckleberry Finn* is a moot point, but, as evidenced by his including it in an anthology of humor that he edited, Mark Twain knew and appreciated "The Expensive Treat."

10. Voyles, 1971, p. 98.

11. Letter of June 1, 1863, from Johnston to Alexander H. Stephens, Alexander H. Stephens Papers, Library of Congress.

12. Voyles, p. 107.

13. Letter of June 26, 1860, to Johnston, Johnston Collection, Georgia Historical Society.

14. Edmund Clarence Stedman, "Literary Estimate of Richard Malcolm Johnston," *Southern History Association Publications,* 2 (October 1898), 315.

15. Henry Mills Alden, "Editor's Literary Record," *Harper's,* 66 (April 1883), 803.

16. Clarence Gohdes, "The Late Nineteenth Century," *The Literature of the American People,* ed. Arthur Hobson Quinn (New York, 1951), p. 652.

17. Alden, p. 803.

18. "The Death of Col. R.M. Johnston," *The* [Baltimore] *Sun,* September 24, 1898, p. 4.

19. Stark Young, "Preface," *Southern Treasury of Life and Literature* (New York, 1937), p. v.

Chapter Three

1. William Howard, "Three Nineteenth-Century Georgia Humorists," Thesis Auburn University 1950, p. 24.

2. Robert L. Phillips, Jr., "The Novel and the Romance in Middle Georgia Humor and Local Color: A Study of Narrative Method in the Works of Augustus Baldwin Longstreet, William Tappan Thompson, Richard Malcolm Johnston, and Joel Chandler Harris," Diss. University of North Carolina, Chapel Hill, 1971, p. 54.

3. Clara Ruth Coleman Wood ("The Fiction of Richard Malcolm Johnston," Diss. University of North Carolina, Chapel Hill, 1973, pp. 224 - 225) enumerates the following counties as those of Middle Georgia: Baldwin, Clarke, Columbia, Elbert, Greene, Hancock, Lincoln, McDuffie, Madison, Morgan, Oconee, Oglethorpe, Putnam, Richmond, Taliaferro, Warren, and Wilkes. Since Johnston identifies Powelton as his village of Dukesborough, Hancock County is at the heart of his fictional world, just as it was of his real one. The actual counterpart of Johnston's working literary area Ms. Wood delineates (p. 202) as the territory within a line drawn clockwise from Athens, along the Broad River, along the South Carolina line, to Augusta, to Milledgeville, and back to Athens.

4. Richard Malcolm Johnston, "Middle Georgia Rural Life," *Century,* 43 (March 1892), 737.

5. Wood, pp. 265 - 266.

6. Wood, p. 266.

7. Probably, as Johnston seems to indicate, all fourteen had appeared previously, but I have not been able to verify such publication either for "Dr.

Hinson's Degree" or "Rev. Rainford Gunn and the Arab Chief."

8. *Mr. Absalom Billingslea and Other Georgia Folk* (New York, 1888), pp. 68 - 69.

9. *Ibid.*, pp. 240 - 241.

10. Quoted in Voyles, 1971, p. 123.

11. Noted in Lessie Brannen Brinson, "A Study of the Life and Works of Richard Malcolm Johnston," Diss. George Peabody 1937, pp. 139 - 140.

12. Voyles, p. 124.

13. Voyles, p. 123.

14. Wood, p. 31.

15. *The Primes and Their Neighbors* (New York, 1891), p. 160.

16. *Ibid.*, p. 158.

17. Similar observations in a more extensive discussion of this story appear in Wood, pp. 122 - 129.

18. *Mr. Fortner's Marital Claims and Other Stories* (New York, 1892), p. 181.

19. *Ibid.*, p. 129.

20. *Ibid.*, pp. 134 - 135.

21. *Ibid.*, p. 2.

22. *Ibid.*, p. 12.

23. *Ibid.*, pp. 11 - 12.

24. Letter of August 17, 1892, from Johnston to E.C. Stedman, Butler Library, Columbia University.

25. *Mr. Billy Downs and His Likes* (New York, 1892), p. vii.

26. Voyles, p. 126.

27. *Mr. Billy Downs and His Likes*, pp. 191 - 192.

28. Brinson, p. 149.

29. *Little Ike Templin and Other Stories* (Boston, 1894), p. 132.

30. *Ibid.*, p. 222.

31. Quoted in Voyles, p. 130.

32. *Old Times in Middle Georgia* (New York, 1897), pp. 15, 17.

33. The titles of the most finished versions of these stories, which exist in manuscript in the Richard Malcolm Johnston Collection at Baltimore's Enoch Pratt Free Library, are "Bella," "Dan and His Friends," "Separation of Friends," "The Vagrant," "Disobedience of Orders," and "A Confederate Rooster." The last two are the most unusual, set during the Civil War and telling of encounters of Southern families with Federal troops.

34. Leona Garner, "A Study of Local Color with Emphasis on Selected Works of Three Georgia Authors," Thesis University of Georgia 1965.

35. "Richard Malcolm Johnston: A Biographical and Critical Study," Diss. University of Georgia 1971.

36. "The Fiction of Richard Malcolm Johnston," Diss. University of North Carolina, Chapel Hill, 1973. This study is to date the most thorough survey of Johnston's work.

37. Diss. University of North Carolina, Chapel Hill, 1971, p. 246.

38. Phillips, p. 309.

39. *Ibid.*

40. *Ibid.*, p. 311.

41. *Autobiography of Col. Richard Malcolm Johnston* (Washington, 1900), pp. 73 - 78.

42. Fred Lewis Pattee, *The Development of the American Short Story* (New York. 1923), p. 276.

43. Carl Holliday, *A History of Southern Literature* (New York, 1906), p. 266.

44. Quoted in Phillips, p. 245.

Chapter Four

1. Johnston regarded *Old Mark Langston, Widow Guthrie,* and *Pearce Amerson's Will* as his three novels, while *Ogeechee Cross-firings* [*sic*] he considered as one of "the stories." Clara Ruth Coleman Wood considers the first two above as long novels and classifies the last two as well as "Mr. Thomas Chivers's Boarder" and "The Pursuit of the Martyns" as short novels.

2. Letter of February 25, 1883, from R.M. Johnston to Alexander H. Stephens, in the Alexander H. Stephens Papers, Library of Congress.

3. *Old Mark Langston: A Tale of Duke's Creek* (New York, 1884), pp. 9 - 11.

4. Regina Armstrong, "Richard Malcolm Johnston, Gentleman and Man-of-Letters," *Catholic World,* 68 (November 1898), 269.

5. C.F. Smith, "Richard Malcolm Johnston" in *Reminiscences and Sketches* (Nashville, Tennessee, 1908), p. 185.

6. These phrases appear in early February, 1884, reviews in the *Atlanta Constitution, New York Tribune, Louisville Evening Post,* and *New York Graphic,* clippings in the R.M. Johnston Collection, Georgia Historical Society.

7. *Ogeechee Cross-Firings* (New York, 1889), p. 55.

8. *Ibid.*, p. 137.

9. *Ibid.*, pp. 75 - 76.

10. Letter of June 2, 1887, from Johnston to Messrs. J.L. and J.B. Gilder, now in Miscellaneous Papers, Manuscripts and Archives Division, The New York Public Library, Astor, Lenox and Tilden Foundations.

11. Letter of November 28, 1889, from Johnston to R.W. Gilder, now in the Century Collection, Manuscripts and Archives Division, The New York Public Library, Astor, Lenox and Tilden Foundations.

12. Letter of December 6, 1889, from R.M. Johnston to Charles Dudley Warner, in the Watkinson Library, Trinity College, Hartford, Connecticut.

13. Letter of November 28, 1889, in the Century Collection, Manuscripts and Archives Division, The New York Public Library, Astor, Lenox, and Tilden Foundations.

14. Letter of October 2, 1890, in the Lilly Library, Indiana University.

15. Voyles, 1971, p. 174.

16. *Widow Guthrie* (New York, 1890), p. 11.
17. *Ibid.*, p. 27.
18. *Ibid.*, p. 114.
19. *Ibid.*, pp. 107 - 108.
20. *Ibid.*, p. 116.
21. *Ibid.*, pp. 190 - 191.
22. *Ibid.*, p. 258.
23. *Ibid.*, pp. 302 - 303.
24. These various judgments come from reviews in *The New York Tribune, The Brooklyn Standard-Union, The New York Sun, The Baltimore Sun,* and *The Christian Union,* excerpted by Appleton's and printed in *The Primes and Their Neighbors.*
25. Voyles, p. 183.
26. *Pearce Amerson's Will* (Chicago, 1898), pp. 226 - 227.
27. *Ibid.*, p. 275.
28. *Ibid.*, p. 237.
29. *Ibid.*, p. 162.
30. *Ibid.*, p. 152.
31. Bernard M. Steiner, "Colonel Richard Malcolm Johnston," *The Conservative Review,* 1 (February 1899), 75.
32. *Pearce Amerson's Will,* p. 113.
33. Jay B. Hubbell, *The South in American Literature, 1607 - 1900* (Durham, N.C., 1954), p. 781.
34. An interview with Johnston printed in the February 24, 1894, *Baltimore Evening Star,* reported in Edna Hendricks, "Richard Malcolm Johnston," Thesis University of Georgia 1936, p. 44.
35. William A. Webb, "Richard Malcolm Johnston" in *Southern Writers: Biographical and Critical Studies,* II (1903; rpt. New York, 1970), p. 81.
36. Letter of March 21, 1890, now in the Department of Archives and Manuscripts, Louisiana State University, Baton Rouge, Louisiana.

Chapter Five

1. Letter of October 2, 1897, now in the William Malone Baskervill Papers, Duke University Library.
2. Letter of September 14, 1888, now in the Butler Library, Columbia University.
3. This first phrase Johnston used in a letter of December 16, 1895, to James Whitcomb Riley, now in the Lilly Library at Indiana University; the second appears in "Some Heroes of Charles Dickens" in *Studies, Literary and Social,* Second Series (Indianapolis, Indiana, 1892), p. 100.
4. Montrose J. Moses, *The Literature of the South* (New York, 1910), p. 461.
5. William A. Webb, "Richard Malcolm Johnston" in *Southern Writers: Biographical and Critical Studies,* II (1903; rpt. New York, 1970), p. 68.

6. Letter of January 13, 1863, now in the Johnston Collection, Georgia Historical Society.

7. R.M. Johnston, "Educational Progress: The Reading Circle as a Factor," *The Catholic Reading Circle Review*, 9 (October 1896), n.p., clipping in the Richard Malcolm Johnston Collection, Enoch Pratt Free Library, Baltimore, Maryland.

8. Lessie Brinson Brannen, "A Study of the Life and Works of Richard Malcolm Johnston," Diss. George Peabody 1937, p. 188.

9. *Ibid.*

10. Letter of February 2, 1874, Alexander H. Stephens Papers, Library of Congress. Manuscripts of the poem are in the R.M. Johnston Collection, Enoch Pratt Free Library, Baltimore, Maryland.

11. Letter of December 29, 1875, Alexander H. Stephens Papers, Library of Congress.

12. Letter of September 27, 1888, Johnston Collection, Georgia Historical Society.

13. Letter of October 1, 1888, from Johnston to E.C. Stedman, Butler Library, Columbia University.

14. Letter of November 3, 1863, Alexander H. Stephens Papers, Library of Congress.

15. Letter of September 27, 1888, Georgia Historical Society.

16. Letter of November 27, 1893, Georgia Historical Society.

17. Voyles, 1971, pp. 189 - 191.

18. Letter of June 25, 1860, from the Reverend Stephen Elliott, to R. M. Johnston, Georgia Historical Society.

19. Letter of September 5, 1860, from J.B. Lippincott to R.M. Johnston, Georgia Historical Society.

20. Letter of June 30, 1870, from J.B. Lippincott to R.M. Johnston, Georgia Historical Society.

21. Letter of September 21, 1871, from R.M. Johnston to A.H. Stephens, Alexander H. Stephens Papers, Library of Congress.

22. Voyles, p. 195.

23. From a clipping in the Johnston Collection, Georgia Historical Society.

24. *Studies, Literary and Social*, First Series (Indianapolis, Indiana, 1891), p. 126.

25. "The Extremity of Satire" in *Studies, Literary and Social*, Second Series, p. 119.

26. *Lectures on Literature: English, French and Spanish* (Akron, Ohio, 1897), pp. 189 - 190.

27. *Ibid.*, p. 269.

28. Letters of November 17, and December 4, 1890, now in the Lilly Library, Indiana University.

29. Letter of September 20, 1891, Lilly Library, Indiana University.

30. Letter of December 4, 1890, from Johnston to James Whitcomb Riley, Lilly Library, Indiana University.

31. *The Century*, 43 (March 1892), 739 - 740.

32. "Richard Malcolm Johnston on Rural Life in Middle Georgia," *Georgia Historical Quarterly*, 58 (Supplement 1974), 183.

33. Stanley J. Kunitz and Howard Haycraft, eds., *American Authors, 1600 - 1900: A Biographical Dictionary of American Literature* (New York, 1938).

34. Andrew James Miller, *Old School Days* (New York, 1900), p. 201.

35. Letter of January 23, 1897, Watkinson Library, Trinity College.

36. *Report of the [U.S.] Commissioner of Education, 1894 - 95*, p. 1702.

37. *Lippincott's*, 47 (March 1891), 401.

38. *Lippincott's*, 61 (June 1898), 862.

39. *Ibid.*, p. 863.

40. *Ibid.*

41. Letter of October 26, 1874, from R.M. Johnston to A.H. Stephens, Alexander H. Stephens Papers, Library of Congress.

42. *Two Gray Tourists* (Baltimore, 1885), p. 53.

43. Quoted in Voyles, p. 208.

44. Voyles, p. 205.

45. Letter of August 11, 1873, from Johnston to A.H. Stephens, Alexander H. Stephens Papers, Library of Congress.

46. *Two Gray Tourists*, p. 274.

47. Letter of April 23, 1869, from Johnston to Stephens, Alexander H. Stephens Papers, Library of Congress.

48. Alexander H. Stephens Papers, Library of Congress.

49. *Autobiography of Col. Richard Malcolm Johnston* (Washington, 1900), p. 183.

50. Manuscript, the Richard Malcolm Johnston Collection, Enoch Pratt Free Library, Baltimore, Maryland.

51. Montrose J. Moses, p. 307.

52. Edd Winfield Parks, "Richard Malcolm Johnston" in *Segments of Southern Thought* (Athens, Georgia, 1938), p. 238.

53. Voyles, p. 200.

54. Parks, p. 238.

55. Letter of November 27, 1880, Alexander H. Stephens Papers, Library of Congress.

56. Parks, p. 223.

57. *Ibid.*, p. 225.

58. The terms are Parks's, p. 244.

Chapter Six

1. Reported in Sophia Bledsoe Herrick, "Richard Malcolm Johnston," *Century*, 36 (June 1888), 276.

2. Cf. Claud B. Green, "The Rise and Fall of Local Color in Southern

Literature," *Mississippi Quarterly*, 18 (Winter 1964 - 65), 1, and Richard Cary, *Mary N. Murfree* (New York, 1967), p. 133.

3. "American Fiction," *The Edinburgh Review*, 173 (January 1891), 53, 51.

4. *Ibid.*, p. 55.

5. Herbert F. Smith, *Richard Watson Gilder* (New York, 1970), [p. 7].

6. *Ibid.*

7. Thomas Wentworth Higginson, "The Local Short Story," *The Independent*, 44 (November 3, 1892), 5.

8. Nathaniel Hawthorne, *Passages from the French and Italian Note-Books*, vol. X, Riverside Edition of *Works* (Boston, 1883), p. 456.

9. Maurice Thompson, "Literary Half-Acres," *The Independent*, 44 (November 3, 1892), 5.

10. *Ibid.*

11. "Local Color and After," *The Nation*, 109 (September 1919), 426.

12. Lee T. Lemon, *A Glossary for the Study of English* (New York, 1971), p. 116.

13. Green, p. 2.

14. George McMichael, *Journey to Obscurity* (Linlcon, Nebraska, 1965), p. 88.

15. See Claude M. Simpson, "Introduction," *The Local Colorists* (New York, 1960), pp. 12 - 15, and Jimmy Ponder Voyles, "Richard Malcolm Johnston's Literary Career: An Estimate," *Markham Review*, 4 (February 1974), 30 - 31.

16. See Robert Underwood Johnson, *Remembered Yesterdays* (Boston, 1923), p. 262, and L. Frank Tooker, *The Joys and Tribulations of an Editor* (New York, 1924), p. 215.

17. "The Death of Col. R.M. Johnston," *The* [Baltimore] *Sun*, September 24, 1898, p. 4.

18. Fred Lewis Pattee, *The Development of the American Short Story* (New York, 1923), p. 276.

19. Walter Blair, *Native American Humor* (1937; rpt. San Francisco, 1960), p. 128; Wade Hall, *The Smiling Phoenix* (Gainesville, Florida, 1965), pp. 15, 23; Clarence Gohdes, "Exploitation of the Provinces" (Chapter 32), *The Literature of the American People*, ed. Arthur Hobson Quinn (New York, 1951), p. 653; F.L. Pattee, *A History of American Literature Since 1870* (New York, 1915), p. 299; Carlos Baker, "Delineation of Life and Character" (Chapter 52), *Literary History of the United States*, ed. Richard E. Spiller et al., 3rd ed. revised (New York, 1963), p. 851.

20. Johnson, *Remembered Yesterdays*, p. 122.

21. Edmund Clarence Stedman, "Literary Estimate of Richard Malcolm Johnston," *Southern History Association Publications*, 2 (October 1898), 316.

22. Fred Lewis Pattee, "The Short Story" (Chapter 6), *Cambridge History of American Literature*, ed. W.P. Trent et al. (New York, 1917), II, 389.

23. Pattee, *History of American Literature*, p. 301.
24. *Ibid.*
25. Joel Chandler Harris, *Stories of Georgia* (New York, 1896), p. 240.
26. Quoted in Paul M. Cousins, *Joel Chandler Harris: A Biography* (Baton Rouge, Louisiana, 1968), p. 9.
27. Pattee, *History of American Literature*, p. 301.
28. Clement Eaton, *The Mind of the Old South*, rev. ed. (Baton Rouge, Louisiana, 1967), p. 131.
29. Jay B. Hubbell, *The South in American Literature, 1607 - 1900* (Durham, N.C., 1954) p. 777.
30. Stedman, p. 315.
31. Carl Holliday, *A History of Southern Literature* (New York, 1906), p. 268.
32. William Dean Howells, *Literature and Life* (New York, 1902), p. iii.
33. See Jimmy Ponder Voyles, "Richard Malcolm Johnston: A Biographical and Critical Study," Diss. University of Georgia 1971, pp. 229 - 230.
34. Letter of December 11, 1894, from W.D. Howells to W. J. Gallery, Richard Malcolm Johnston Collection, Enoch Pratt Free Library, Baltimore, Maryland.
35. "Recent Fiction," *The Dial*, 25 (July 1, 1898), 22. Italics mine.
36. Edd Winfield Parks, "Richard Malcolm Johnston" in *Segments of Southern Thought* (Athens, Georgia, 1938), p. 243.
37. "Introduction," *Autobiography of Col. Richard Malcolm Johnston* (Washington, 1900), p. 6.
38. Parks, pp. 238 - 239.
39. Letter of December 24, 1874, from Johnston to Alexander H. Stephens, Alexander H. Stephens Papers, Library of Congress.
40. Letter of July 4, 1889, Butler Library, Columbia University.
41. *Autobiography*, p. 85.
42. "Speech at Atlanta, Georgia, State Fair, August, 1857," manuscript in the Richard Malcolm Johnston Collection, Enoch Pratt Free Library, Baltimore, Maryland.
43. Merrill Maguire Skaggs, *The Folk of Southern Fiction* (Athens, Georgia, 1972), p. 119.
44. Letter of December 11, 1888, from Johnston to James Whitcomb Riley, Lilly Library, Indiana University.
45. Parks, p. 239.
46. William A. Webb, "Richard Malcolm Johnston" in *Southern Writers: Biographical and Critical Studies*, II (1903; rpt. New York, 1970), p. 80.
47. Bernard M. Steiner, "Colonel Richard Malcolm Johnston," *The Conservative Review*, 1 (February 1899), 74-75.
48. Parks, p. 244.
49. *Ibid.*, p. 225.
50. *Ibid.*, p. 244.

Selected Bibliography

1. Original Materials

The three largest and most important manuscript collections relating to Johnston are those bearing his name at the Enoch Pratt Free Library in Baltimore and the Georgia Historical Society in Savannah, and the Alexander H. Stephens Papers in the Library of Congress. Smaller but still valuable Johnston holdings, primarily letters, may be found in manuscript collections at Duke University, Emory University, Trinity College (Johnston to C.D. Warner correspondence), Columbia University (Johnston to E.C. and Arthur Stedman), Indiana University (Johnston to J.W. Riley), and the New York Public Library (Johnston to R.W. Gilder).

2. Books

The English Classics: A Historical Sketch of the Literature of England from the Earliest Times to the Accession of King George III. Philadelphia: J.B. Lippincott and Company, 1860.

[Philemon Perch, pseud.] *Georgia Sketches.* Augusta, Georgia: Stockton and Company, 1864.

[Philemon Perch, pseud.] *Dukesborough Tales.* Baltimore: Turnbull Brothers, 1871.

[with William Hand Browne] *English Literature: A Historical Sketch of English Literature From the Earliest Times.* New York: University Publishing Company, 1872.

[Philemon Perch, pseud.] *Dukesborough Tales.* Second Enlarged Edition. Baltimore: Turnbull Brothers, 1874.

[with William Hand Browne] *Life of Alexander H. Stephens.* Philadelphia: J.B. Lippincott and Company, 1878.

Dukesborough Tales. New York: Harper and Brothers, 1883.

Old Mark Langston: A Tale of Duke's Creek. New York: Harper and Brothers, 1884.

Two Gray Tourists: From Papers of Mr. Philemon Perch. Baltimore: The Baltimore Publishing Company, 1885.

Mr. Absalom Billingslea and Other Georgia Folk. New York: Harper and Brothers, 1888.

Ogeechee Cross-Firings: A Novel. New York: Harper and Brothers, 1889.

Widow Guthrie: A Novel. New York: D. Appleton and Company, 1890.

The Primes and Their Neighbors: Ten Tales of Middle Georgia. New York: D. Appleton and Company, 1891.
Studies, Literary and Social. First Series. Indianapolis: The Bowen-Merrill Company, 1891.
Dukesborough Tales: The Chronicles of Mr. Bill Williams. New York: D. Appleton and Company, 1892.
Mr. Billy Downs and His Likes. New York: Charles L. Webster and Company, 1892.
Mr. Fortner's Marital Claims and Other Stories. New York: D. Appleton and Company, 1892.
Studies, Literary and Social. Second Series. Indianapolis: The Bowen-Merrill Company, 1892.
Little Ike Templin and Other Stories. Boston: Lothrop Publishing Company, 1894.
Lectures on Literature: English, French and Spanish. Akron, Ohio: D.H. McBride and Company, 1897.
Old Times in Middle Georgia. New York: The Macmillan Company, 1897.
Pearce Amerson's Will. Chicago: Way and Williams, 1898.
Autobiography of Colonel Richard Malcolm Johnston. Washington: The Neale Company, 1900.

3. Essays, Articles, Poem
    The following list is far from exhaustive for Johnston's nonfiction prose. What appears here are those uncollected pieces that have the most biographical, historical, or literary value. The two volumes of *Studies, Literary and Social* bring together a total of twenty essays or articles, none of which is noted here.
"Religious Intoleration." *DeBow's Review,* 22 (February 1857), 166 - 180.
"Wind of the Winter Night." *The Southern Magazine,* 7 (March 1874), 309 - 311. [poem]
"Reading Bores." *Lippincott's,* 47 (March 1891), 401 - 403.
"Middle Georgia Rural Life." *Century,* 43 (March 1892), 737 - 742.
"My Schools." *Lippincott's,* 54 (November 1894), 703 - 708.
"Early Educational Life in Middle Georgia." Chapter 42, pp. 1699 - 1733, Volume 2, *Report of the* [United States] *Commissioner of Education for the Year 1894 - 95.* Washington: Government Printing Office, 1896.
"Early Educational Life in Middle Georgia." Chapter 16, pp. 839 - 886, Volume 1, *Report of the* [United States] *Commissioner of Education for the Year 1895 - 96.* Washington: Government Printing Office, 1897.
"The Planter of the Old South." *Southern History Association Publications,* 1 (January 1897), 35 - 44.
"Dogs and Railroad Conductors." *Lippincott's,* 61 (June 1898), 862 - 864.
"The Conversion of Richard Malcolm Johnston. As Related by Himself." *Truth* (April 1899), 3 - 6.

SECONDARY SOURCES

1. Books
   Heretofore no book has been devoted exclusively to Richard Malcolm Johnston. The following list includes some which provide a short but meaningful introduction / orientation to the man and his works or which comment significantly if briefly on his place in American literary history. Not noted here are the standard histories of American literature or reference books of American biography; the many exclusively Georgia or exclusively Southern reference books of history and biography, many of which have an informative if overly loving entry on Johnston; or the many literary collections or anthologies, Southern and otherwise, that reprint Johnston's work, often with a lengthy headnote.

BEALE, ROBERT CECIL. *The Development of the Short Story in the South.* Charlottesville, Virginia: The Mitchie Company, 1911. A brief but judicious characterization of Johnston's "stories of 'Cracker' life"; regards *Georgia Sketches* as a very important contribution to the Southern short story in "a period of transition."

BLAIR, WALTER. *Native American Humor.* 1937; rpt. San Francisco: Chandler Publishing Company, 1960. Contains a recognition of Johnston's important transitional position and associates him in this regard with Mark Twain.

EATON, CLEMENT. *The Waning of the Old South Civilization, 1860 - 1880s.* Athens: University of Georgia Press, 1968. Regards Johnston as the most important postbellum local-color humorist for a study of the mores of Southern folk.

FOSTER, RICHARD ALLEN. *The School in American Literature.* Baltimore: Warwick and York, 1930. High, deserved credit granted to Johnston within the context of this significant subject and theme in American literature.

HALL, WADE. *The Smiling Phoenix: Southern Humor from 1865 to 1914.* Gainesville: University of Florida Press, 1965. Sees Johnston as "the writer who best illustrates the changing humor of the Civil War period" and, significantly, associates him with the postbellum literary vogue of looking at life through the eyes of a child.

HERRON, IMA HONAKER. *The Small Town in American Literature.* Durham, North Carolina: Duke University Press, 1939. As in the Foster book but here more critically, Johnston is given praise within the framework of a significant subject and theme of American literature.

HOLLIDAY, CARL. *A History of Southern Literature.* New York: The Neale Publishing Company, 1906. An example of an early attempt at a scholarly evaluation of Johnston; some important recognitions but some misinformation and too glowing a final assessment.

HUBBELL, JAY B. *The South in American Literature, 1607 - 1900.* Durham, North Carolina: Duke University Press, 1954. Contains a good assimilative introduction to and a perceptive evaluation of Johnston and his works; special attention given to the man's personality and his relationship with other Southern writers.

PARKS, EDD WINFIELD. *Segments of Southern Thought*. Athens: University of Georgia Press, 1938. Chapter 12, "Richard Malcolm Johnston," the finest twenty-one consecutive pages on Johnston in existence.

PATTEE, FRED LEWIS. *The Development of the American Short Story: An Historical Survey*. New York: Harper and Brothers, 1923. Concise discussion of Johnston's sudden rise and later decline as a writer in favor; sees him "in one respect [the evolution of *Dukesborough Tales*] a notable figure in the history of the short-story form," but in all other respects, only a "type-representative" of a large number of transitory writers of local color.

———. *A History of American Literature Since 1870*. New York: The Century Company, 1915. A helpful placing of Johnston within the successive regional literary vogues, especially the Southern; asserts that "Johnston was to the Southern movement what Eggleston was to the Western."

SKAGGS, MERRILL MAGUIRE. *The Folk of Southern Fiction*. Athens: University of Georgia Press, 1972. Johnston diffusedly viewed and evaluated in terms of "a literary tradition [the plain folk] which heretofore has not been recognized as a part of the southern heritage."

SMITH, CHARLES FORSTER. *Reminiscences and Sketches*. Nashville, Tennessee: Publishing House of the Methodist Episcopal Church, South, 1908. Number 9 of these collected papers (written in 1892) an appealing sketch of Johnston by one who knew him personally, and a critical overview of his literary works by one who knew what was praiseworthy in them.

TOOKER, L. FRANK. *The Joys and Tribulations of an Editor*. New York: The Century Company, 1923. Contains a charming anecdotal description of Johnston by this *Century* editor who took an "extraordinary delight" in him.

WEBB, WILLIAM A. *Southern Writers: Biographical and Critical Studies*. Vol. II. 1903; rpt. New York: Gordian Press, 1970. The Johnston "study" an informative, sympathetic but well-balanced treatment of the man and his works.

2. Articles

ARMSTRONG, REGINA. "Richard Malcolm Johnston, Gentleman and Man-of-Letters." *The Catholic World*, 68 (November 1898), 261 - 270. An article of tribute that reproduces important family photographs; focuses on Johnston's expression of his concept of a gentleman.

BUSH, ROBERT. "Richard Malcolm Johnston's Marriage Group." *Georgia Review*, 18 (Winter 1964), 429 - 436. Tries to establish the social value of Johnston's fiction by looking at his persistent theme of courtship and marriage.

COLEMAN, CHARLES W., JR. "The Recent Movement in Southern Literature." *Harper's New Monthly Magazine*, 74 (May 1887), 837 - 855. A contemporary look at Johnston and his place in the great surge of interest in Southern literature in the 1880s.

EDWARDS, CORLISS HINES, JR. "Richard Malcolm Johnston's View of the Old Field School." *Georgia Historical Quarterly*, 50 (December 1966), 382 - 390. Simply a calling of attention to the pervasive topic of schools and education in Johnston's works.

EDWARDS, HARRY STILLWELL. "A Reminiscence of Richard Malcolm Johnston." *The Atlanta Journal*, June 13, 1933, p. 8. A delightful account of Johnston's return to the semi-centennial celebration of Mercer University in Macon, Georgia, in 1883.

GAVIGAN, WALTER V. "Two Gentlemen of Georgia." *The Catholic World*, 145 (August 1937), 584 - 589. A short "review" of the life and works of Johnston and Joel Chandler Harris, "fellow converts to the Catholic faith."

HERRICK, SOPHIA BLEDSOE. "Richard Malcolm Johnston." *The Century Illustrated Monthly Magazine*, 36 (June 1888), 276 - 280. An article that gave Johnston wide exposure at the time; informative if extremely appreciative of the man and his work.

LONG, FRANCIS TAYLOR. "Part I of The Life of Richard Malcolm Johnston in Maryland, 1867 - 1898: Country Gentleman, Teacher, and Writer, 1867 - 1881." *Maryland Historical Magazine*, 34 (December 1939), 305 - 324.

————. "Part II of The Life of Richard Malcolm Johnston in Maryland, 1867 - 1898: Some Literary Friendships—The Lecture Platform, 1882 - 1889." *Maryland Historical Magazine*, 35 (September 1940), 270 - 286.

————. "Part III of The Life of Richard Malcolm Johnston in Maryland, 1867 - 1898: The Closing Years, 1889-1898." *Maryland Historical Magazine*, 36 (March 1941), 54 - 69. Very valuable and detailed study by a scholar who long planned a full-length biography of Johnston and who had gained the confidence of Johnston's last surviving daughter and literary executor.

PARKS, EDD WINFIELD. "Professor Richard Malcolm Johnston." *Georgia Historical Quarterly*, 25 (March 1941), 1 - 15. A valuable and detailed account of Johnston's association with the University of Georgia, drawn from documents in the University archives.

"Richard Malcolm Johnston." *The Dial*, 25 (October 1, 1898), 213 - 215. A sincere, extended tribute to Johnston—"novelist, scholar and gentleman"—soon after his death.

STEDMAN, EDMUND CLARENCE, and STEPHEN B. WEEKS. "Literary Estimate and Bibliography of Richard Malcolm Johnston." *Southern History Association Publications*, 2 (October 1898), 315 - 327. Despite some errors of fact and overgenerous critical acclaim, an essential starting-point document for a study of Johnston.

STEINER, BERNARD M. "Colonel Richard Malcolm Johnston." *The Conservative Review*, 1 (February 1899), 74 - 77. A reminiscent, impressive posthumous tribute to Johnston by a friend and admirer.

VOYLES, JIMMY PONDER. "Richard Malcolm Johnston's Literary Career: An Estimate." *The Markham Review*, 4 (February 1974), 29 - 34. Exposition and argument proving that Johnston "because of his accomplishments deserves consideration three generations later as an author of historical significance."

3. Theses and Dissertations

Johnston and his works have been the subjects of scrutiny in a surprising number of doctoral dissertations and, particularly, master's theses. Some, especially the most recent ones, are significant contributions to knowledge; others, especially some early theses, are appallingly deficient and sometimes blatantly dishonest.

BRINSON, LESSIE BRANNEN. "A Study of the Life and Works of Richard Malcolm Johnston." Dissertation, George Peabody College for Teachers, 1937. A helpful study which concludes, however, that Johnston's "literary achievements should be recognized as those of an artist in a restricted realm."

EYLER, CLEMENT MANLY. "Richard Malcolm Johnston and His *Dukesborough Tales*." Thesis, Columbia University, 1926. Noteworthy mainly because of Eyler's claim of personal interviews with some of Johnston's Middle Georgia models.

GARNER, LEONA. "A Study of Local Color with Emphasis on Selected Works of Three Georgia Authors." Thesis, University of Georgia, 1965. Johnston considered along with Joel Chandler Harris and Harry Stillwell Edwards in a general-through-specific look at local color.

HOWARD, WILLIAM. "Three Nineteenth-Century Georgia Humorists: A Comparative Study of the Writings of Augustus Baldwin Longstreet, William Tappan Thompson, and Richard Malcolm Johnston." Thesis, Auburn University, 1950. A solid, well-researched study which emphasizes Johnston's "transition from realism to idealized concept."

MCKAY, ANNE LECONTE. "A Comparison of *Dukesborough Tales* by Richard Malcolm Johnston with *Georgia Scenes* by Augustus Baldwin Longstreet." Thesis, Mercer University, 1950. Probably most valuable simply for the suggestiveness of its particular limited topic.

PHILLIPS, ROBERT L., JR. "The Novel and the Romance in Middle Georgia Humor and Local Color: A Study of Narrative Method in the Works of Augustus Baldwin Longstreet, William Tappan Thompson, Richard Malcolm Johnston, and Joel Chandler Harris." Dissertation, University of North Carolina at Chapel Hill, 1971. Shows that the literature by Johnston and these other writers indicates that, despite their claims, they "were not willing to examine and expose the area and its people with consistent realistic honesty."

PITTMAN, FRANCES HARRIS. "Middle Georgia Life in the Fiction of Richard Malcolm Johnston." Thesis, Duke University, 1941. Tries to show that Johnston faithfully reproduces the characters and customs of the late 1830s and '40s in Middle Georgia.

VOYLES, JIMMY PONDER. "Richard Malcolm Johnston: A Biographical and Critical Study." Dissertation, University of Georgia, 1971. An important scholarly contribution, made so largely but not exclusively by Voyles's thorough study of the Johnston to Alexander Stephens letters.

WOOD, CLARA RUTH COLEMAN. "The Fiction of Richard Malcolm Johnston." Dissertation, University of North Carolina at Chapel Hill, 1973. A significant categorization and critical discussion of all of Johnston's fiction; sees Johnston not as a great but as an important Southern writer, a storyteller concerned essentially with *charm*.

WOOD, JAMES WYATT. "Richard Malcolm Johnston." Thesis, University of South Carolina, 1931. A well-balanced consideration with some important biographical facts.

Index

Alden, Henry M., 55, 126, 139
American Copyright League, 41, 128, 132, 133

Bird, Edgeworth, 36, 121
Brown, Gov. Joseph E., 24, 34
Browne, William Hand, 29, 37, 40, 112, 122, 123 - 25

Cable, George Washington, 43, 134
Civil War, 30, 33 - 34, 62, 73, 75, 82, 129, 146n33
Colonel Carter of Cartersville (F. Hopkinson Smith), 56, 133

Dawson, Edgar, 36, 121
Dickens, Charles, 112 - 13

Edwards, Harry Stillwell, 131, 133, 135
Eggleston, Edward, 128, 134, 136

Festus (Philip James Bailey), 43, 109
Frost, A. B., 95, 110

Georgia, University of, 25, 26 - 30, 42, 93, 117
Gilder, Richard W., 97 - 98, 139

Harris, George Washington, 56
Harris, Joel Chandler, 23, 42, 68, 134 - 35
Hooper, J. J., 27, 49, 134
Howells, William Dean, 120, 130, 133, 136 - 37, 139

Johnston, Catherine (mother), 16 - 17
Johnston, Malcolm (father), 15 - 16, 19
Johnston, Mary Frances M. (wife), 19 - 20, 29, 32, 35, 36, 42, 43, 95, 96
Johnston, Richard Malcolm, as literary critic, 110 - 14; as public platform

figure, 25, 41 - 42, 113, 115, 128, 133, 136, 138; as university professor, 26 - 30; as young schoolteacher, 18, 19, 20 - 21; birth and ancestry, 15 - 16; childhood and early education, 17; children, 15, 20, 30 - 31, 34 - 35, 36, 38, 39, 43; college education, 17 - 18; conversion to Roman Catholicism, 38; death, 43; early reading, 106; European travel, 37, 119 - 22; government employment, 35, 42 - 43; honorary degrees, 42; ideas on education, 28, 31 - 32, 36; involvement in politics, 23 - 24, 122 - 23; legal practice, 18, 19, 21 - 23, 25, 30; marriage, 19 - 20; on his literary efforts, 42, 87 - 88, 108, 109; publication in Catholic journals, 113, 116; residence in Baltimore, 39 - 43; residence at "Pen Lucy," 36 - 39; residence at "Rockby," 31 - 35; unpublished pieces, 84, 109 - 10, 146n33; use of "Philemon Perch" pseudonym, 37, 45 - 47, 119 - 22, 136

WORKS—FICTION:
"Adventure of Mr. Joel Boozle, An," 77
"Almost a Wedding in Dooly District," 78 - 79
"Bachelor's Counselings, A," 78
"Beazley Twins, The," 48, 64
"Bee Hunters, The," 81
"Black Spirits and White," 81
"Brief Embarrassment of Mr. Iverson Blount, The," 70
"Buck and Old Billy," 81
"Campaign of Potiphar McCray, The," 80, 81, 82
"Careful Pleadings," 81
"Case of Spite, A," 83

160